MATHEMATICS TEACHING CASES

Fractions, Decimals, Ratios, and Percents

WRITING COLLABORATORS

Susan Aitken

Richard Bevacqua

Debra Coggins

Leslie Crenna

Gail Dawson

Sue Dirlam

Rosita Fabian

Judy Flores

Sharon Friedman

Joann Fuller

Donna Goldenstein

Rosalyn Haberkern

Amy Hafter

Susan Hennies

Bernadette Homen

Babette Jackson

Bruce Jackson

Kathleen Lloyd

Rose Lock

Jennifer McConnell

Joanne Matala

Eric Moskowitz

Judy Norman

Barbara Polito

Alma Ramirez

Lee Tempkin

David Thornley

Kim Tolley

Hardy Turrentine

Ricki Wortzman

Daniel Zimmerlin

The people listed above contributed to the development of the cases. Although each case has a primary author, all of them were collaboratively framed and revised. We have therefore not cited the author of each case individually. Furthermore, all names in the cases have been changed to protect the identity of the students, teachers, and schools portrayed therein.

Fractions, Decimals, Ratios, and Percents

Hard to Teach and Hard to Learn?

Edited by

Carne Barnett
*Far West Laboratory for Educational Research
and Development*

Donna Goldenstein
Hayward Unified School District

Babette Jackson
Hayward Unified School District

Heinemann
Portsmouth, NH

Heinemann
A division of Reed Elsevier Inc.
361 Hanover Street
Portsmouth, NH 03801-3912

Offices and agents throughout the world

Every effort has been made to contact the copyright holders for permission to reprint borrowed material where necessary. We regret any oversights that may have occurred and would be happy to rectify them in future printings of this work.

The authors/editors and publisher wish to thank those who have generously given permission to reprint borrowed material:

"On the Pulse of Morning" by Maya Angelou. © 1993 by Maya Angelou. Reprinted by permission of Random House, Inc.

This publication is funded by Stuart Foundations and based on work supported by the U. S. Department of Education, Office of Educational Research and Improvement, contract number 400-86-0009. Its contents do not necessarily reflect the views or policies of Stuart Foundations, or the Department of Education, nor does the mention of trade names, commercial products, or organizations imply endorsement by our sponsoring agencies.

Library of Congress Cataloging-in-Publication Data

Fractions, decimals, ratios, and percents: hard to teach and hard to learn? / edited by
   Carne Barnett, Donna Goldenstein, Babette Jackson.
     p. cm.—(Mathematics teaching cases)
   Includes bibliographical references.
   ISBN 0-435-08357-0.—ISBN 0-435-08358-9 (facilitator's discussion guide)
   1. Fractions—Study and teaching (Elementary) 2. Ratio and proportion—Study and teaching (Elementary) I. Barnett, Carne. II. Goldenstein, Donna. III. Jackson, Babette. IV. Title: Hard to teach and hard to learn? V. Series.
QA117.F698 1994
372.7'2—dc20   94-19983
                                                                                  CIP

Editor: Toby Gordon
Production: Vicki Kasabian
Text design: Catherine Hawkes
Cover design: Darci Mehall

Printed in the United States of America on acid-free paper
09 08 07 06   VP   10 11 12

Contents

Inside Student Thoughts

Making Sense or Memorizing Rules?

Connections

This Wasn't My Plan

Foreword

The publication of this volume of cases remarkably improves the prospects for a vigorous era of case-based teacher education and professional development. Carne Barnett, collaborating closely with two teacher-leaders from Hayward Unified School District, Donna Goldenstein and Babette Jackson, has given us a powerful new model of teacher-written cases. These accounts illustrate typical problems that occur in the classroom teaching and learning of fundamental albeit frequently misunderstood mathematical ideas. Unlike most other casebooks, which confront the difficulties of managing classrooms, relating to kids, or finding one's way through the complexities of teaching in a complex organization without referring to specific subjects, this casebook takes the mathematics curriculum as its starting point and the teacher's subject-specific instructional responsibilities as its focus.

Veteran teachers understand that when students leave behind the safe harbor of operations on whole numbers and enter the abyss of fractions, decimals, ratios, and percents, problems ensue ("stuff happens"). Students who have previously succeeded begin to falter, their confidence wanes, failures increase, and teachers despair. The problem is not only that students distrust their own mathematical intuitions, but also many elementary school teachers find themselves in unfamiliar territory, skating tentatively on the thin ice of their own limited mathematical understanding. This unease often leads to routinized pedagogy, procedure-ridden assignments, and falling morale. Recent studies of teachers' responses to the new mathematics frameworks in California and elsewhere attest to the great difficulties teachers are facing in attempting to teach mathematics for understanding, enjoyment, and use.

Barnett and her colleagues build on the traditions we have begun in Far West Laboratory's Institute for Case Development by attacking this dilemma using the most effective (and underused) resources educators possess—the stories, insights, experiences, and voices of teachers themselves. Classroom teachers have come together during the past three years to share their accounts of mathematics teaching with one another. Under Carne's thoughtful guidance, they have explored these accounts and identified those that most usefully exemplify the recurring dilemmas of math teaching that bedevil teachers and impair their effectiveness in fostering student understanding. The teachers who have collaborated in this effort have written those stories in the form of "teaching cases" designed to stimulate their colleagues to examine their own practice, to think hard about the mathematics they teach and would like to teach, and to initiate inquiries and discussions that lead teachers to a deeper understanding of student thinking and the kinds of strategies that would promote further learning.

The teacher-written cases have been selected, organized, and edited (always in close collaboration with the teacher-authors themselves) with an eye to connecting them thematically to the growing body of research on mathematical learning. Respect for the importance of the teacher's voice need not come at the expense of recognizing the value of more formal research and theory in mathematics education. For example, deeply held student misconceptions about mathematical relations often lie at the heart of pedagogical difficulties. Many of these cases rest on detecting and confronting such misconceptions. Other cases vividly portray the often overlooked impact of language use on mathematical learning. Thus, in this volume's first case, when the teacher asks the students to "take one-third of one and one-third ($\frac{1}{3}$ of $1\frac{1}{3}$)" the ambiguities of our commonsense uses of *take* help to obscure the underlying mathematical operations and lead to unanticipated difficulties. Both student misconceptions and the role of language have been subjects of extensive research among mathematics educators.

The typical case reports a problem, dilemma, or crisis of mathematics instruction that has occurred in a teacher's class. Something the teacher planned has gone awry—whether a "problem of the day," an attempt to get students to represent critical concepts, or an effort to help students recognize the beauty of mathematics. Students have become confused, have utterly missed the point, or have grown upset with the teacher's efforts to assist them. And the teachers have reached a point where they just don't know what to do. The case describes the events that led up to the problem, the classroom context in which it occurred and the ways in which the teacher attempted to set matters on course. It often also includes the teacher's own analyses of the situation and the emotional impact of the problem.

Some might argue that these accounts of teachers' misunderstandings or miscues risk adding to the shameful practice of "teacher bashing," that national sport in which teachers are favorite targets for those purporting to explain all the ills of American education. That is a fundamental misreading of this casebook and all others like it. These are cases written by and for teachers, not about them. They represent the highest manifestation of professional responsibility for reflecting on one's own practice, analyzing its weaknesses, and learning from experience. Such learning from one's own and others' experience is made possible only when critical reflections on practice engage the attention of professionals and when the resulting analyses are made public and voluntarily shared with peers. The result is far from teacher bashing; it is the essence of mature professional learning.

These cases and the accompanying facilitator's discussion guide have been extensively field-tested. Groups of teachers have read and discussed the cases and have wrestled with the issues of content and pedagogy that inhere within each of them. The most impressive feature of this research is that Carne has demonstrated that the teachers have learned significant aspects of both mathematics and its teaching from their work with the cases and from the discussion of the cases with their fellow teachers.

Carne Barnett, Donna Goldenstein, Babette Jackson, and the nearly thirty teacher colleagues who contributed to this volume have paved the way for a new generation of case materials for teacher education and professional development. We anticipate many more curriculum-specific casebooks over the coming years, in which teachers construct vivid accounts of the tough problems and small victories of teaching the central ideas of their subjects to students of different backgrounds across many school contexts. These materials will be invaluable as educators around the world attempt to transform the educational process into a more constructive force to enhance student understanding and critical thinking. The Far West Laboratory and the Institute for Case Development are proud to be associated with this pioneering contribution.

Judith H. Shulman, *Far West Laboratory*
Lee S. Shulman, *Stanford University*

Preface

Getting Hooked on Cases

Anyone interested in mathematics teaching and learning is likely to get hooked on case discussions. The mental stimulation and the chance to discuss practical and theoretical problems with others is appealing and gratifying. In fact, in our experience the attraction to cases is so strong that teachers have begun to organize and initiate their own discussion groups.

Our cases are narratives written by classroom teachers. Narratives are powerful, not only because they *relate* experiences, but also because they *create* experiences. The intriguing plots of these cases, which occur in classrooms every day, stimulate our emotions and capture our imaginations. One purpose of this collection of cases is to illustrate problematic situations that will evoke thoughtful analyses and reflection about teaching and learning. A second purpose of this casebook is to enable teachers to build their own mathematical knowledge as it relates to real classroom situations. Our ultimate hope is that these processes will become long-term and self-sustaining within the culture of the school and the classroom.

This casebook and the accompanying facilitator's discussion guide are the result of several years of teachers and researchers learning together. My own involvement began as a teacher educator at the University of California, Berkeley, working in collaboration with a project directed by Lee Shulman at Stanford University. The first case prototypes were developed by teachers from Vallejo Unified School District. This work was expanded through the Mathematics Case Methods Project, which began as a collaboration between Far West Laboratory and Hayward Unified School District and has since been adopted by several other sites as well.

When we first started in 1987, we had no model for subject-specific teaching cases. Teachers simply wrote about their experiences teaching fractions, decimals, ratios, or percents—topics often considered hard to teach and hard to learn. They wrote about successful and unsuccessful experiences that surprised, disappointed, or puzzled them. The cases were then field-tested as a means of stimulating discussion among groups of teachers. Whether short and focused or longer and more elaborate, the cases fostered complex discussions about mathematics teaching, discussions that few teachers had previously experienced. The beauty of this approach is that it provides a new way of fostering teacher learning that both draws on and informs their practice.

This casebook and the accompanying facilitator's discussion guide, developed at Far West Laboratory, are the first in a series that will be developed for mathematics teachers. Far West Laboratory has also developed other casebooks for educators and has been on the cutting edge of case methodology for several years. The laboratory also offers seminars for educators interested in learning how to develop or use cases.

Links to Mathematics Education Reform

The cases in this book carry no presumption that the teaching they portray is either good or bad. Case discussion participants must decide for themselves the benefits and drawbacks of various approaches and are thus more likely to claim ownership of the ideas and to change their teaching practices accordingly.

The cases do contain illustrations of many ideas advocated by reform documents such as the National Council of Teachers of Mathematics' (NCTM) *Curriculum and Evaluation Standards for School Mathematics* (1989) and *Professional Standards for Teaching Mathematics* (1991). For example, they highlight alternative assessment methods, the use of manipulatives, the relevance of language and writing, connections among mathematical ideas, calculator use, and invented algorithms. The table of contents lists two or three of the most salient NCTM *Standards* topics for each case. The facilitator's discussion guide reviews specific issues related to these topics.

The suggested readings for each case, culled primarily from books and journals published by NCTM, provide additional perspectives relevant to that particular case. These readings are designed to trigger further thought, not to give answers. The issues raised in the readings should be open to as much debate as the issues that emerge from the case. We also suggest that you read, or reread, the introduction of this casebook as another means to orient yourself with this approach to professional development.

Casebook Audience

These cases were created by fourth- through eighth-grade teachers and therefore will be most appropriate for teachers of those grades. However, many teachers from primary and secondary schools have told us that the cases were stimulating for them as well. Primary teachers gain insight into the mathematics that their students are being prepared to learn, and secondary teachers gain an appreciation for the dilemmas and complexities of teaching faced by teachers in earlier grades. Teachers in grades K–12 have found that the cases have provided them with insight into teaching at their grade levels.

All the cases have been extensively field-tested with inservice teachers, and selected cases were field-tested with preservice teachers. Although the casebook was originally created as a tool to foster the professional growth of practicing teachers, we have found that it also holds promise for preservice teachers. Our preliminary studies show that even with little or no classroom experience, preservice teachers had in-depth discussions and targeted many of the same issues discussed by practicing teachers.

Using the Casebook

These cases are written to stimulate collaborative reflection through discussion. Group interactions enable one to consider alternative perspectives and question the status quo.

There are many ways to form discussion groups. Participants may come from many schools or districts, or they may be from a single school faculty. Both compositions have their strengths and weaknesses. If meeting together on a regular basis is difficult, teachers may have conversations about the cases with colleagues over electronic networks. No matter the approach taken, case discussions are more successful when they are offered as an option rather than specified as a requirement.

If it is not possible or feasible to join a discussion group, the next best thing is to read the casebook in conjunction with the facilitator's discussion guide, interacting with the ideas found there. The discussion guide provides extensive teaching notes for each case, designed to help the facilitator anticipate issues he or she might capitalize on in the discussion. They highlight the major issues that will potentially arise and provide background information about these issues as necessary. (For specific guidance about conducting case discussion groups, refer to the facilitator's guide.)

Carne Barnett, *Far West Laboratory*

Acknowledgments

A number of teachers have devoted considerable time and creative energy to this project. I admire their courage in writing candidly about their teaching situations, knowing that the cases would be open to critical analysis by others. Nevertheless, they revealed their thoughts, their problems, and their sometimes flawed decisions so that others might learn. The cases and case discussion process evolved through the thoughtful suggestions given by all of the teachers involved.

The ideas, support, and encouragement of Professor Lee Shulman at Stanford University have been instrumental in the development of this casebook and facilitator's discussion guide. He is responsible for bringing both the case technique and pedagogical content knowledge to the forefront of our thinking in teacher education, and thus provides the inspiration for our work. I am grateful for the vision that Lee provides as a member of our advisory board, and I especially appreciate the personal interest he shows by getting to know teachers in the project and using the cases in his own courses.

I am also indebted to the co-editors of this casebook, Donna Goldenstein and Babette Jackson, for reviewing the manuscript and participating in the revision process. They organized and nurtured the collaboration between Hayward Unified School District and Far West Laboratory that made this work possible. More importantly, they knew how to tap the wisdom of teachers to ensure the credibility and practicality of this work.

Others who have guided the case development process include the members of our advisory board, listed in the appendix. Their thoughtful contributions have been invaluable. In addition, I want to acknowledge my colleagues at Far West Laboratory. Judy Shulman's work provided the first models for teacher-authored cases and inspired me to pursue the same level of quality. Pam Tyson shares the project responsibilities with me, and I greatly value her perspective and in particular her contribution to the discussion guide. The administrative assistants for this project, Cary Raglin and Leslie Crenna, put their hearts and hard work into preparing the casebook for publication. The publication was also enhanced by the professional work of editors Joan McRobbie and Joy Zimmerman.

Teacher to Teacher: Introduction to Cases

Not What We Expected

Amy Hafter, *Hayward Unified School District*
Kathleen Lloyd, *Hayward Unified School District*

When we were first introduced to case discussions, we were expecting a traditional math inservice in which a presenter instructs participants in his or her philosophy or teaching approach. We expected suggestions for using manipulatives or new problems and activities for our students. What we actually received was very different.

Before the first discussion, we were given a story—a case—of another teacher's actual classroom experience to read and reflect on. As a formal lead-in, we were then asked to work in pairs to generate questions prompted by the case. These questions were written on butcher paper and used to stimulate the whole-group discussion.

We soon found out that each case raised different issues, some controversial, some merely puzzling. In one case discussion, for example, we tried to figure out the relative limitations of using money or base-10 blocks to teach decimals. In another, we discussed why a teacher might have deliberately posed a problem that was confusing to students.

At first we weren't sure if the discussion was on the right track. Were we covering the important points? Were there specific answers to these questions? As the discussions continued we came to realize that there was rarely one "right" answer, and that as participants, we were responsible for the quality and content of the discussions. The facilitator was not an expert, but a guide.

Initially many of us worried about being "politically incorrect" or about exposing our limited experience with math or new methods of teaching. Others were more assertive, offering all kinds of ideas for teaching the concepts discussed in each case. As discussions progressed, we slowly came together as a group, developing mutual trust and building an environment in which all opinions were respected yet open to debate. The fact that the cases were anonymous allowed for more open and honest discussion.

On reflection, we also see parallels between what we experienced as learners in the case discussions and the kind of learning we want to promote in our own classrooms. Through the case discussions we became involved in problem solving, open-ended discussions, and real-world applications—exactly what we want for our own students. Perhaps one of the most important outcomes of these discussions was the learning community that evolved among veteran and novice teachers together. The bond we forged helped to eliminate the feelings of isolation and inadequacy so common in our profession.

What to Expect from Case Discussions

Becky Hemann, *Hayward Unified School District*
Alma Ramirez, *Jingletown Charter Middle School, Oakland*
Norma Sakamoto, *Hayward Unified School District*

We, as teachers, realize how important it is to know the relevance of any undertaking before we invest our valuable time. The following summary attempts to address or mediate the difficulty in explaining the value of the process of case discussions. Its purpose is not to condemn other forms of professional development but to provide a contrast. We hope it offers a framework that will guide your own case discussions.

What to Expect	What Not to Expect
Collaborative reflection on common dilemmas and questions about teaching	Responding to dilemmas and questions of practice all by yourself
A chance to discuss compelling classroom stories in order to find common ground among teachers with diverse experiences	Ready-made lesson plans and activities
A long-term process that develops mutual trust, wisdom, and support among colleagues	A quick cure-all with no follow-up support
A chance to analyze student thinking in depth to maximize learning experiences	A generic approach that overlooks students' ideas and experiences
An opportunity to become your own change agent by critically analyzing and adapting resources and methods	Top-down professional development conducted by an outside expert
An opportunity to wrestle with mathematical concepts and to see them through the eyes of students	A workshop that focuses on materials and overlooks students' mathematical thinking

Fractions, Decimals, Ratios, and Percents

Inside Student Thoughts

*Guidance is not external imposition. It is freeing the
life-process for its own most adequate fulfillment.*

JOHN DEWEY

Take One-Third

As my seventh and eighth graders entered our classroom and found their seats, their attention turned to the "starter problem" written on the overhead. I asked them to work on it silently in preparation for the day's lesson on multiplying fractions.

> *On your own, draw a picture where you take $\frac{1}{3}$ of $1\frac{1}{3}$. Hint: Start with a picture of $1\frac{1}{3}$.*

I finished administrative tasks as the students worked, then walked around to look at their pictures. I decided to ask Linda and Bob to show their solutions on the board, so that I could illustrate the use of both continuous and discrete fractions. We turned first to Linda's picture.

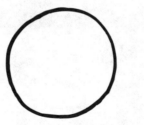 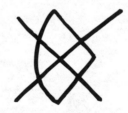

"How did you start the problem, Linda?"

"I just drew 1 and $\frac{1}{3}$," she said.

"So this circle represents a whole, and this piece is $\frac{1}{3}$ of another equal-sized whole?"

"Yeah."

Several students commented that they had drawn very similar pictures. I asked Linda to explain how she solved the problem.

"I just took away $\frac{1}{3}$ from 1 and $\frac{1}{3}$," she answered, as she crossed out the $\frac{1}{3}$.

"Listen to what you just said," I prompted.

"I just took away $\frac{1}{3}$ from 1 and $\frac{1}{3}$," Linda insisted.

"What operation did you say out loud?" I asked.

"Take away—subtraction."

When I directed her attention back to the problem on the overhead, she looked confused, saying: "Take $\frac{1}{3}$ of $1\frac{1}{3}$. I don't get it. This is weird."

Still hoping the class would be able to discover the proper procedure on its own, I switched to Bob, expecting that his solution would be both correct and easier for the class to understand.

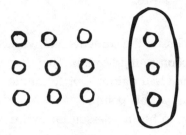

He explained how he started. "I thought of 9 spots being in the whole and then 3 more would be $\frac{1}{3}$."

"So how did you find $\frac{1}{3}$ of $1\frac{1}{3}$?"

"I just took $\frac{1}{3}$," he replied, indicating three of the spots.

"You should take 4," Jim and a few other students cried out. I asked them to think about what it means to take $\frac{1}{3}$, giving a hint by pointing to the denominator.

"Divide them into 3 equal groups," Amanda volunteered, "and you get 1 of those groups or $\frac{1}{3}$."

Then I attempted a real life example that would relate Bob's problem to the previous day's lesson. I asked them to imagine that Bob's items were popsicles and to think about $\frac{1}{3}$ of all of them. Bob could get one part, his brother another equal part, and his mom another third. His dad is on a diet. How many popsicles would it be fair for Bob to eat? Jane and several students said 4, a few said 3. I called on Jane to explain.

"$\frac{1}{3}$ of 12 is 4. You just divide," she replied.

"So we weren't supposed to take away $\frac{1}{3}$. These are division problems," Max realized. "Why didn't you tell us?" The whole class was a little unhappy with my "deception."

All this took place in a general math class in a medium-sized suburban middle school with 850 students. There were twenty seventh graders and six eighth graders in the class. I had chosen fractions as one of my teacher-evaluation curricular areas for the year.

I had begun the unit by giving a pretest on basic fraction concepts and operations, including some word problems. Because the scores were on average very low, I decided to spend a couple of months working with these ideas so my students would show substantial growth on the post-test.

We spent the first few weeks developing meaning for fractions, placing a strong emphasis on being able to draw a picture of a fraction amount. Most pictures showed subdivisions in rectangles, with number lines being used occasionally. I offered examples of work with discrete fractions, such as $\frac{12}{24}$ meaning 12 of the 24 original pieces of candy in a box, which in turn means the box is half full. By the time we reached the current lesson, the students also had some experience drawing representations of subtraction problems such as:

$$\frac{1}{2} - \frac{3}{8}$$

On the day before this lesson the students had worked on pictures that introduced the concept of fraction multiplication. They had sketched problems such as $\frac{1}{3}$ of 27 pieces of gum and had figured $\frac{1}{4}$ of 16 candies. The word *multiplication* had not been formally used at this point.

So here we were trying to begin a lesson on multiplying fractions, and now Linda's work had revealed that she thought we were talking about subtraction. Then, from Bob's example the class had impulsively concluded that "you just divide." I wondered if it had been a mistake to follow my usual custom of having students experiment with a new concept on their own before the formal lesson. Was it practical—or possible—to capitalize on these misunderstandings and proceed with the lesson? Or should I have started over and approached the lesson by giving a little more guidance?

I now see that similarities in the language of multiplying and subtracting fractions call for a careful choice of words. But beyond that, my own understanding of fractions has been shaken by Max's statement. It seems that you do divide when multiplying fractions. But how am I going to make sense of that to my students?

Suggested Readings

Borasi, R. 1990. "The Invisible Hand Operating in Mathematics Instruction: Students' Conceptions and Expectations." In *Teaching and Learning Mathematics in the 1990s*, edited by T. J. Cooney and C. R. Hirsch, 174–182. Reston, VA: The National Council of Teachers of Mathematics.

Miller, L. D. 1993. "Making the Connection with Language." *Arithmetic Teacher* 40(6): 311–316.

Beans, Rulers, and Algorithms

I n my fifth/sixth-grade class, we have been working with fractions since the beginning of the year. The students basically understand what a fraction is and how to add and subtract fractions with common denominators. We have worked with finding equivalent fractions as well as reducing them, looked at improper fractions and mixed numbers, and used a variety of manipulatives. The students clearly were able to complete problems with pencil and paper.

After an assessment of these areas, I felt we were ready to move ahead to adding with different denominators. We took out 12 beans. Students first separated them into 2 equal groups to show $\frac{1}{2}$. Next, they drew pictures to show how many beans equal $\frac{1}{2}$. We then recombined all 12 beans and separated them into 3 equal groups to show thirds, again drawing pictures. We followed the same process for fourths, sixths, and twelfths.

We went through several addition problems with this drawing now complete, then added problems such as $\frac{1}{3} + \frac{3}{12}$. The students were able to look at the drawing they had made in order to figure how many beans would equal $\frac{1}{3}$ and how many would equal $\frac{3}{12}$. We practiced with drawings. Students very quickly felt comfortable with the process.

$$\frac{1}{3} \;+\; \frac{3}{12} \;=\; \frac{7}{12}$$

We also looked at rulers, reviewing how an inch is divided into fractional parts. We added $\frac{1}{2}$ and $\frac{5}{16}$. The students were able to locate $\frac{1}{2}$ on the inch ruler and then add $\frac{5}{16}$ to $\frac{1}{2}$ and correctly find the answer.

$$\frac{1}{2} + \frac{5}{16} = \frac{13}{16}$$

Such experiences went on for a couple of weeks. But when I then demonstrated this adding process on paper, we ran into trouble. I taught them a couple of ways to find common denominators and change them so the fractions could be added. To my frustration, they switched from understanding the concepts to memorizing a formula. It was clear that once we left the manipulatives, many students did not understand adding with different denominators.

My lower students simply added the numerators and added the denominators to get an answer.

$$\frac{1}{6} + \frac{2}{7} = \frac{3}{13}$$

Other students knew to multiply by a common factor to make common denominators but made errors in the process.

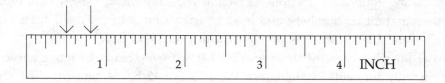

$$\times 7 \left(\frac{1}{6} + \frac{2}{7} \right) \times 6$$
$$\frac{7}{42} + \frac{6}{42} = \frac{13}{42}$$

And there were still others who could add the numbers correctly but had no understanding of why it worked to multiply the numerator and denominator by the same number.

Now I am left with questions. Should I be satisfied if the students can use a formula to solve the fraction problem, even if they don't understand the theory behind it? Should I continue until they understand why what they are doing works? Should I allow them to continue using manipulatives? Where should I go from here?

Suggested Reading

Yackel, E., P. Cobb, T. Wood, G. Wheatley, and G. Merkel. 1990. "The Importance of Social Interaction in Children's Construction of Mathematical Knowledge." In *Teaching and Learning Mathematics in the 1990s*, edited by T. J. Cooney and C. R. Hirsch, 12–21. Reston, VA: The National Council of Teachers of Mathematics.

There's No One-Half Here

I had been using cube blocks with my fifth graders to demonstrate the concept of multiplying fractions, such as $\frac{2}{3} \times 6$. First, I'd have students take 6 cubes and lay them on the table. Next, I'd ask them to divide their cubes into thirds. Finally, I'd ask them to pick up $\frac{2}{3}$ and be ready to tell me how many they were holding. After a lot of practice, students could easily demonstrate the following types of problems.

$$\frac{3}{8} \times 32$$

$$\frac{4}{5} \text{ of } 40$$

Several days later, I decided to use the cubes again to demonstrate problems like $\frac{3}{4} \times \frac{1}{2}$. I asked students to take 8 cubes and set them on the table. I asked them to pick up $\frac{1}{2}$ of the cubes, which they quickly did. Next, I asked them to show me $\frac{3}{4}$ of the $\frac{1}{2}$ they were holding. Immediately, I sensed confusion everywhere.

"Mrs. Tinley, what do you mean, '$\frac{3}{4}$ of the $\frac{1}{2}$ we're holding?'" asked one girl. "We're holding 4 cubes, not $\frac{1}{2}$."

Suggested Reading

Witherspoon, M. 1993. "Fractions: In Search of Meaning." *Arithmetic Teacher* 40(8): 482–485.

Everything I Know About Decimals

Part One

As I began my third year of teaching, I looked with dread at our sixth-grade math text. The first chapter was on place value and, of course, decimals followed that. I had agonized over the summer about how I was going to approach decimals and thought back to my first two years of teaching. My first year, I had been handed a box of manipulatives and a math text. I used them to the best of my ability. I had also participated in a program that introduced me to cooperative groups and provided curriculum units for bilingual students. I was satisfied with the enthusiasm the materials generated, and to my untrained eye it seemed that important decimal concepts had been learned through these methods. The second year, I joined a math-case discussion group to see if I could expand my repertoire to fractions and percents.

The case discussions really led me to a level of frustration that is difficult to explain. By talking with teachers in higher grade levels, I found out that our kids, even by high school, have very little understanding of fractions, decimals, ratios, and percents. As a bilingual teacher I had already noticed that children from Latin America who had been to school there usually excelled in math, yet most of our native-born Chicano and African American students were, year after year, failing dismally in this area. I joined the educators who feel our whole approach to teaching these populations must be rethought. The more I read, however, the more I began to feel that the teaching of math had to change for everyone. I finished the second year determined to try something new with decimals and fractions—and my whole math program.

I began the next year still undecided about what that something new was going to be, hoping that by attending case discussions I could figure it out. A moment of realization came when I read a case that questioned whether the use of manipulatives could also become rote learning.

At that time, I had already started my decimal unit. We focused on decimal place value and how to read and write decimal numbers. I used a manipulative that depicted decimals with "whole squares," which were made of cardboard, and each "whole" was predivided into smaller squares to represent tenths, hundredths, or thousandths. Students looked at the shaded part of a whole square to determine which decimal was represented. The more I thought about it, the more I questioned how much thinking or understanding was being generated through these manipulatives. To name the decimal represented by the graphic below, for example, students simply had to count the number of shaded squares (32) and give the name for the number of smaller squares in the larger whole square (hundredths). The decimal would be "32 hundredths."

I asked myself, whether they really understood that a decimal was part of a whole, or were they merely parroting responses based on visual comparisons rather than reasoning?

I decided to find out what they knew about decimals so far and asked them to explain in writing "everything you know about decimals." Ana's explanations were fairly representative of most of her classmates' explanations.

Ana's journal

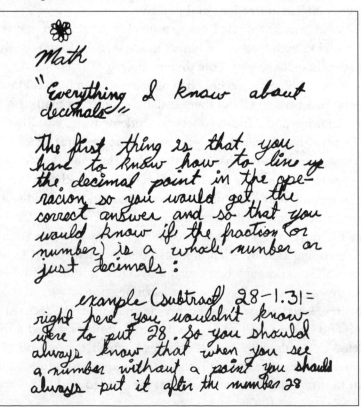

Math

"Everything I know about decimals"

The first thing is that you have to know how to line up the decimal point in the operacion so you would get the correct answer and so that you would know if the fraction (or number) is a whole number or just decimals :

example (subtract) 28 – 1.31 =
right here you wouldn't know were to put 28 . So you should always know that when you see a number without a point you should always put it after the number 28

I immediately stopped what I had started because I knew this wasn't the path I wanted to take.

Part Two

After much contemplation, I decided to use the metric system as a tool for teaching decimals. Since most of my students are immigrants, they were already familiar with metric measurement. I considered its strengths: The metric units are conveniently divided into multiples of 10; the units go to the thousandths, which money does not do; it is used in science; and more importantly for me, what they would measure was not predivided as the decimal square units were.

What I hoped to accomplish was the development of number sense through measurement. In general when children memorize place-value charts, they really don't get a sense of the relative "size" or magnitude of tenths, hundredths, or thousandths. I found that this could be accomplished to some extent with decimal square units or base-10 blocks with my students but the amount of time they spent mentally or physically manipulating the materials was limited. As a result, they often performed the addition and subtraction algorithms "forgetting" to line up the decimals or putting the smaller number on "top" without giving it a second thought.

Once I had decided that I was going to use metric, it fell in nicely with my two science measurement units. I began by having the children make meter sticks out of paper and asked them to keep them for the duration of the unit. First, they divided the paper meter into 10 equal pieces by folding and drew a vertical line at each fold. Next, they divided each tenth into 10 equal parts, to make hundredths. Then I had them use estimation to divide the hundredths into ten parts to make thousandths. (Because it was so tedious, I asked them to divide only one 10 cm part into thousandths.) The meter was our "whole," and the divisions represented decimal parts of that whole.

At first we practiced drawing lines that were a given length, such as 0.24 m long or 0.3 m long, to help them become familiar with decimal notation. Then we did lots of estimation activities. After a few days of these experiences, I asked them to find the difference between their estimates and the real measures. Without any instruction, many children were able to subtract the decimals. They even figured out how to subtract when the estimates and measures did not have the same decimal places. I didn't have to mention a word about lining up the decimals. They just did it because it made sense to them. It became a game to see how close they could come to a difference of zero.

This decimal unit spanned about two and a half months. I focused on using measurement to teach what I felt was important—estimation, problem solving, logic, number sense in terms of the value of place, and the "size" of things.

Teaching decimal computation, in my mind, was only important insofar as it helped to accomplish the previous goals.

I was also trying new methods of assessing students and gave them an assignment to find out what they had learned about decimals. I asked them to write ten things they knew about decimals and to include specific examples. Since their work was to be placed in their portfolios, the children were especially careful. On the following pages you see Ana's work (her journal was presented earlier), Orlando's work, Helena's work, and John's work. I would say that their responses were representative of the range of work done by the majority of the class.

Ana's work

merth Homework

What I Know
aboot decimals

① I learned that there are 100 cm in a meter and there are 1000 mm in a meter

② I learned that $\frac{9}{10} = .9$

③ I learned thet when you are going to x or + or − if there are 4 numbers ofter the decimal Point that you need to coute 4 or more numbers ofter the decimal Point.

$$23.\boxed{42}$$
$$\times 58.\boxed{10}$$
$$\overline{2360.7020}$$

④ I Know that $\frac{1}{1,000}$ is more smaller than $\frac{1}{100} = .01$

Ana's work (continued)

⑤ I learned that to the leaft is the Whole number and to the right is part of a number
whole 24.086 part

⑥ I learned the place value and how to do problems of decimals.

hundred	tens	ones	tenth	hundredth
3	4	5	1	0

$$345.10$$
$$\times \ \ 10.10$$

⑦ I knew that I need to line up the decimals because you could get confuse with which number you did to x, + or —.

$$2.08$$
$$+\ 0.86$$

$$2.08$$
$$+\ 0.80$$
$$\overline{12.88}$$

⑧ I know that mm are smaller than cm and cm are more smaller than a meter.

⑨ I learned how to do from a fraction to a decimal.
$$\frac{1}{100} = .01$$

⑩ I know that 4 parts out of 10 something is equal 400 parts of 1000 of something. Example

Although Orlando's work is in Spanish, you may be able to see that he has learned algorithms for adding, subtracting, and multiplying (his first three examples). He can also write the symbols and names for one whole, one tenth, and one hundredth (his fourth example). In example 5, he demonstrates an ability to compare decimal numbers, even though the number of places in these decimals varies.

Orlando's work

Matemáticas

① Yo se sumar con puntos decimales

25.95

$25.95 + 128.44 = 154.39$ ← $+128.44 =$
$\overline{154.39}$

Primero pongo los puntos uno arriba y otro abajo y después

pongo los números como están y empieso a sumar

② Yo se restar con puntos decimales

$29 - 24.08 = 04.92$ 29.00

Aqui deveria pongo $-24.08 =$
$\overline{04.92}$

los puntos uno arriba y otro abajo y en el primer punto pongo ade-
lante del punto 29 y después atras del punto pongo dos ceros por
es un numero entero   y vuelve a restar

③ Yo se multiplicar con puntos decimales.

$222 \times 2.2 = 488.4$ 222

Aqui acomodo los números como $2.2 =$
$\overline{444}$
Cuando estoy multiplicando por 444
$\overline{488.4}$

y ya que multiplique todo veo cuantos lugares del punto hay
y se lo pongo ④ cuando acabo de hacer todo
Yo se leer los numeros decimales-

1. ➡ Un entero
.1 ➡ Un decimo
.01 ➡ un cien

⑤ Se comparar los numeros decimales que son más chicos
y mas grandes. $.95 > .877$

$.60 = .6$

$.25 < .7$

On this page of Orlando's portfolio work he shows that he knows the fraction equivalencies for the decimals .7, .05, and .002 (his sixth example), and he knows the decimal equivalent for $\frac{1}{4}$ in relationship to a whole (his seventh example). In his final examples, he drew diagrams of meter sticks to illustrate his understanding of the decimal relationships in the metric system. He states that there are 10 tenths in a meter (his eighth example), 100 centimeters in a meter (his ninth example), and 10 centimeters in a decimeter (his tenth example).

Orlando's work (continued)

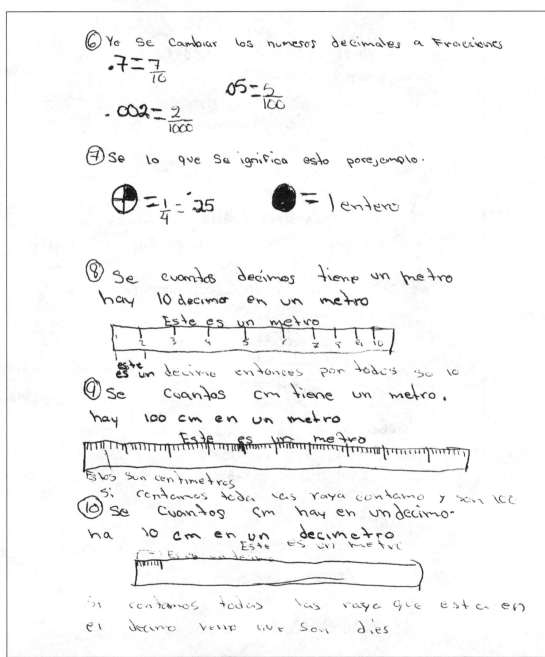

Although Helena could only think of seven things to write about, her writing shows she is becoming familiar with the relationships between fractions and decimals, and she can represent both fractions and mixed numbers as decimals.

She demonstrates some of these equivalencies with drawings. She also talks about measuring with decimals and shows the values of a decimal place-value chart.

Helena's work

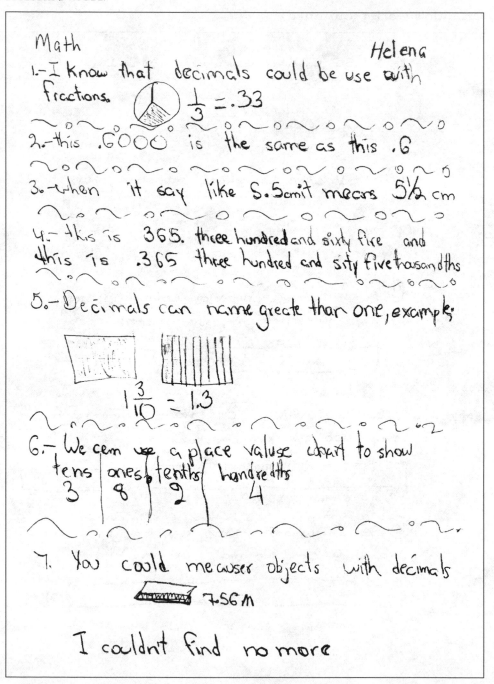

I am also including John's paper. He didn't even attempt the journal-writing assignment earlier in the year. As you can see, John has severe writing and language problems. He is a resource student and attends special classes. Although it takes a little work to interpret his writing, notice that he begins with an example of decimal place value. He then illustrates his knowledge of fraction and decimal equivalency, decimal and percent equivalency, and equivalency between different forms of decimals (.1 = .10). Finally, he states that decimals are part of a number and that he learned how to read decimals.

John's work

As I look through the thirty-two portfolios for my class, I ask myself: "What do my students now know? Are there still 'holes' in the unit or in their learning? How do I have time to delve through all of this, and what do I do with the information it brings?"

Epilogue

My experience as a teacher is very limited, and I don't feel as secure as I'd like with the unknown. My consolation is that it can't hurt to try. The old way does not work for most Latino or African American children. Actually, I'm not sure it works for most children.

Of course, some kids still do not "get it." Some still have to work on the development of critical-thinking skills. And, although most students are on task and enjoy the manipulation of objects, minds, and bodies, some are uncomfortable with the lack of exact answers.

I am still plagued by the idea that I am not drilling the kids on pages of fractions and decimals and 2-or-3 digit whole number division. After all, this is what gets tested on the computation part of standardized tests, right? There is no room on these tests to walk around the room and measure or to write all that they've learned. Where does all this fit in?

But I am gaining confidence. For example, my students are about to be given the sixth-grade math placement test for our district. As I was reviewing the test format with them and going over some sample test problems, I asked the kids not to use a pencil. We were going to try to figure out 3-digit multiplication, division (with and without decimals), fractions, and some problem solving by using our heads. After some prompting about the kinds of things to look for, I gave them a sample test with no scratch paper. More than half of the class finished 15 problems in less than 8 minutes. Somewhere, someone must be doing research on the possibilities of taking these tests using a logical rather than computational approach. For now, I think I'm starting to do the right thing for my kids.

Suggested Reading

Cuevas, G. 1990. "Increasing the Achievement and Participation of Language Minority Students in Mathematics Education." In *Teaching and Learning Mathematics in the 1990s*, edited by T. J. Cooney and C. R. Hirsch, 159–165. Reston, VA: The National Council of Teachers of Mathematics.

Holmes, E. E. 1990. "Motivation: An Essential Component of Mathematics Instruction." In *Teaching and Learning Mathematics in the 1990s*, edited by T. J. Cooney and C. R. Hirsch, 101–107. Reston, VA: The National Council of Teachers of Mathematics.

Secada, W. G. 1990. "The Challenges of a Changing World for Mathematics Education." In *Teaching and Learning Mathematics in the 1990s*, edited by T. J. Cooney and C. R. Hirsch, 135–143. Reston, VA: The National Council of Teachers of Mathematics.

Steen, L. A. 1990. "Mathematics for All Americans." In *Teaching and Learning Mathematics in the 1990s*, edited by T. J. Cooney and C. R. Hirsch, 130–134. Reston, VA: The National Council of Teachers of Mathematics.

How Can 100% of Something Be Just One Thing?

Several months ago, I was reviewing some math concepts with my top fifth and sixth graders. They were preparing to compete in the California League Mathematics Contest in March, and we were practicing by working on some problems from previous years' tests. I put the following problem on the board and asked them to choose the correct answer.

$$100\% = \text{A.} \quad 10$$
$$\text{B.} \quad 1$$
$$\text{C.} \quad 100$$
$$\text{D.} \quad \frac{1}{100}$$

Everyone in the group chose C, which surprised me. "Why did you choose C?" I asked.

"Well, because if 100% of the people took the test, then all 100 were there," answered a sixth-grade girl. Everyone nodded.

"Does 100% mean that there always have to be 100 people or things?" I began to see doubt on some faces.

"Noooo," said Eric, a fifth grader. "If I get 100% on the science exam, there aren't 100 problems. There might only be 15 or 20." They wanted to know the right answer.

"Maybe you could change 100% into a fraction," I said.

They did this mentally, and all seemed to agree that the answer would be $\frac{100}{100}$. Then I suggested reducing the fraction to lowest terms.

"$\frac{1}{1}$ . . . Oh, that's 1."

There was silence for a moment as everyone digested this. "But Mrs. Thomas," asked Crystal, "that doesn't make sense, does it? How can 100% of something be just one thing?"

I believe my students, who are from a low-income, ethnically diverse community, should be prepared for competition in contests such as this one. One goal is to help them spot the "tricky questions," but a more important goal is to ensure that they truly understand concepts, such as percents. Clearly they needed additional experiences, but what kind?

Suggested Reading

Allinger, G. D., and J. N. Payne. 1986. "Estimation and Mental Arithmetic with Percent." In *Estimation and Mental Computation*, edited by H. L. Schoen and M. J. Zweng, 141–155. Reston, VA: The National Council of Teachers of Mathematics.

Making Sense or Memorizing Rules?

Knowledge emerges only through invention and re-invention, through the restless, impatient, continuing, hopeful inquiry [we] pursue in the world, with the world, and with each other.

PAULO FREIRE

Point Seven plus Point Four Is Point Eleven

After fifteen years of teaching, students' errors can still take me by surprise. For several weeks this fall I taught a unit on decimal fractions to my average seventh-grade math class. Although they had all been taught decimals in elementary school, I was aware of many gaps in their knowledge. I thought perhaps some solid work on the meaning of decimals would help bridge some of those gaps. I began by emphasizing the meaning of place value, using both fraction and money examples. I was particularly picky about students reading decimal numbers properly—.6 as "6 tenths" rather than "point 6"—in the hopes of reinforcing place-value meaning and connecting it to the students' knowledge of fractions. After some time, even my slower students were able to express decimals as fractions and give money examples for decimals, both in writing and orally. I was feeling pretty good.

As we moved into addition, to help students avoid problems with such things as lining up the decimals I continued to emphasize the meaning of the individual places as well as the value of the entire decimal. I did many parallel problems on the board using fractions, decimals, and dollars and cents, and then had the students do similar problems at their desks. They seemed to have little difficulty and were soon doing problems like these on their own.

$$
\begin{array}{cccc}
.3 & \overset{1}{.27} & .83 & .4 \\
+\,.5 & +\,.58 & +\,.51 & +\,.35 \\
\hline
.8 & .85 & 1.34 & .75 \\
\end{array}
$$

We discussed their work, and everyone seemed to understand the problems. Things were going well, so I assigned a worksheet with a variety of decimal addition exercises for homework.

When we went over the homework the next day in class, I called on several students to put their work on the board as I walked around the room checking the work of others. All was going well until we came to what I thought was a very simple problem. Several of my students, including Troy who was quite bright, Melissa who tended to drift, and my underachiever J. J., had all made the following mistake.

$$\begin{array}{r} .7 \\ +.4 \\ \hline .11 \end{array}$$

I was taken aback. They had done fine on much harder problems, even multidigit with carrying! I asked Troy to explain how he had done the problem.

"Oh, it's obvious. Point 7 plus point 4 is point 11," Troy responded.

"After all we've done, he still doesn't know his place value!" I thought.

"But what does that mean?" I asked. "Suppose that was money. Then point 7 would be 7 dimes. Right?"

"I guess so," he said.

"And point 4 would be 4 dimes. So how much money is that? $1.10, right?"

Troy looked doubtful but seemed to agree. The rest of the class was getting restless so I had to move on to other things, but I'm still confused about that error. I thought they had grasped place value, but had they really? And why was their lack of understanding revealed on that problem and not on more difficult ones?

Suggested Reading

Hiebert, J. 1984. "Children's Mathematical Learning: The Struggle to Link Form and Understanding." *The Elementary School Journal* 84(5): 497–513.

Hiebert, J. 1992. "Mathematical, Cognitive, and Instructional Analyses of Decimal Fractions." In *Analysis of Arithmetic for Mathematics Teaching*, edited by G. Leinhardt, R. Putnam, and R. A. Hattrup, 283–322. Hillsdale, NJ: Lawrence Erlbaum Associates.

Janvier, C. 1990. "Contextualization and Mathematics for All." In *Teaching and Learning Mathematics in the 1990s*, edited by T. J. Cooney and C. R. Hirsch, 183–193. Reston, VA: The National Council of Teachers of Mathematics.

Schielack, J. F. 1991. "Reaching Young Pupils with Technology." *Arithmetic Teacher* 38(6): 51–55.

I Still Don't See Why My Way Doesn't Work

My eighth-grade basic math class had been reviewing the year's work in preparation for the final exam. We had taken several practice tests, each covering various parts of the material. One student, Glen, who had begun the year slowly but picked up interest and made greater progress during the second semester, had made several errors on the test section covering multiplication of fractions. I went over the relevant rules with the whole class and we did some additional problems. All the students, including Glen, seemed to understand the rules and used them well.

After class Glen came up to me and said, "I understand the rules you gave in class really well, but what I don't understand is why my way doesn't work."

"What way are you using?" I asked.

"Well, with a problem like $6\frac{3}{4} \times 5\frac{1}{3}$, I multiply 6 × 5 to get 30, then $\frac{3}{4} \times \frac{1}{3}$ to get $\frac{3}{12}$, so my answer would be $30\frac{1}{4}$. But that's wrong and I don't see why."

"Why did you do the problem that way?"

"Because in addition and subtraction you do the wholes and the fractions separately. I figured you could do the same with multiplication."

Glen seemed to be genuinely confounded by this inconsistency and wanted to talk about it, so I invited him to drop by at lunch or after school. As he left for his next class, I wondered if he would show up. He did, and I began by writing the same problem on the board, $6\frac{3}{4} \times 5\frac{1}{3}$. "What does this mean?" I asked.

"I don't know . . . $6\frac{3}{4} \times 5\frac{1}{3}$ . . . What else?"

"Okay. Does that mean the same as 6 × 5 plus $\frac{3}{4} \times \frac{1}{3}$?"

"I don't know . . . Why not?"

"When you separate them the way you did, you end up multiplying the 6 by just the 5. Shouldn't the 6 be multiplied by the $\frac{1}{3}$ as well?"

We began to write down the problem now, multiplying 6 × 5, 6 × $\frac{1}{3}$, 5 × $\frac{3}{4}$, and $\frac{3}{4} \times \frac{1}{3}$. "Now add all these answers. What do you get?"

"It reduces to . . . $32\frac{48}{12}$ . . . 36."

"Now let's see what happens when we try the method we used in class. Change both mixed numbers to improper fractions and then multiply numerators and then denominators. What do you get?"

"$\frac{27}{4} \times \frac{16}{3}$, if I cross cancel it's 9 × 4. That's 36." He seemed somewhat surprised that the two methods produced the same answer.

He started to leave the classroom but suddenly turned and said, "But wait a minute. I still don't see why my way doesn't work."

I told him it was because he only multiplied the whole numbers by themselves and not by the fraction part as well. "You need to do both, as we did when we worked the problems out separately," I added lamely, knowing that I hadn't really answered his question.

"Oh, I see," Glen said with a lack of conviction. I told him to think it over and see me again if he still had questions.

Suggested Reading

Janvier, C. 1990. "Contextualization and Mathematics for All." In *Teaching and Learning Mathematics in the 1990s*, edited by T. J. Cooney and C. R. Hirsch, 183–193. Reston, VA: The National Council of Teachers of Mathematics.

The Decimal Wall

Boy, was I caught by surprise toward the end of a rather simple lesson on rounding decimals. Based both on my students' proficiency in rounding whole numbers and their many experiences with place-value concepts, I expected an easy transfer into decimal rounding. I thought my sixth-grade students seemed quite ready to use symbols rather than manipulatives to estimate with decimal numbers.

Before this lesson, I had given my class many informal experiences geared toward developing concepts in whole numbers and decimal place values. They had counted, looked for patterns, and played games using the hundreds and hundredths charts. Using money, they had practiced counting from a cent to more than a dollar. They had used graph paper and also base-10 blocks to name and compare whole numbers and decimals.

Judging from their journal writing and our class discussions, I felt they had attained a fairly solid understanding of place value. For example, when I posed the question, "Tell me all you can about the number 4.16," these were some of their responses:

"It's close to 4.20."

"It's between 4.15 and 4.17."

"It could mean $4.16."

"Four units and $\frac{16}{100}$."

"It could be a swimming record."

"Part wholes, part fraction."

Joey went to the board and drew this picture:

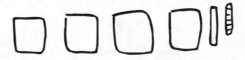

Rounding with whole numbers had also been covered extensively, and students had attained a high level of success with a low level of frustration.

After two days of introducing decimal rounding (to the nearest whole number, tenths, and hundredths places) using base-10 blocks and numerous money examples, I gave an assignment involving rounding decimals on their own, without using manipulatives.

As I walked around the class to assess students' work, I noticed that all the answers on Nazia's paper were correct, except for a problem in which she was trying to round the digit 9 upward. When instructed to round the number 5.895 to the nearest hundredth, Nazia had written 5.810. I asked Nazia, an average student, to explain her answer.

"Well, since I'm rounding to the hundredths place I really need to look at the thousandths place," she said, while accurately pointing to both places, "and since that's a 5 I need to round up the hundredths place, so that makes the 9 a 10."

I was taken aback, yet curious to know how many others shared that thinking. We continued from the board with the same example.

Hoping my students wouldn't agree, I asked for a "thumbs up" response. To my disappointment, several of my average students gave me the "thumbs up." I just had to pursue their thinking, so I asked them to consider a second problem.

"How many of you would say 5,895 to the nearest ten is 5,810?" All thumbs pointed to the floor. It just didn't make sense.

I began to wonder. Why was it that a student such as Nazia, who could round 395 to 400 and $3.95 to $4.00, could not round .395 to .40? In later discussions with teachers, the idea of the "decimal wall" dawned on me: A concept well understood without a decimal point becomes cumbersome when a decimal point is added. But how *do* we go about knocking down the "decimal wall?" How might I help them use what they already know about rounding with whole numbers to make sense of rounding decimals?

Suggested Reading

Baroody, A. J. 1989. "Manipulatives Don't Come with Guarantees." *Arithmetic Teacher* 37(2): 4–5.

Knocking Off Zeros

This year my average sixth-grade class spent the first several months of school working on fractions. We used many concrete materials including fraction kits, plastic cubes, the kids in the class, and base-10 blocks as our concrete models. The set of base-10 blocks we used was made up of flats, longs, and units.

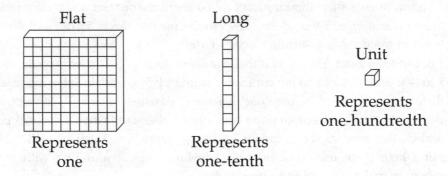

Flat

Represents
one

Long

Represents
one-tenth

Unit

Represents
one-hundredth

When using the base-10 blocks, the students discovered they could "knock off zeros" to simplify, instead of dividing the numerator and denominator by the greatest common factor. They made this discovery by seeing the relationship with the blocks.

Twenty units is the same as two longs, so
twenty hundredths is the same as two tenths

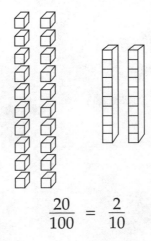

$$\frac{20}{100} = \frac{2}{10}$$

I was pleased about the discovery and thought it was fine to use the "knock-off zeros" short cut rather than divide numerator and denominator by 10. It never occurred to me that they would remember the knock-off part and forget all they had learned about equivalent fractions and simplifying fractions.

In mid-January, I had the class design a floor plan for a house on a 10 by 10 grid. Then I asked them to figure out both a simplified fraction and a percent to show what part of the house was represented by each room. Since the grid had 100 squares, they could simply look at the fraction written with 100 in the denominator and the numerator would be the percent. So for a room that had an area of 24 square units, they would write:

$$\frac{24 \div 4}{100 \div 4} = \frac{6}{25} = 24\%$$

Most kids had little trouble. However, some of my students, like Tom, used the following method.

Bedroom $\frac{15}{100} = \frac{1}{10} = 1\%$

Bathroom $\frac{2}{100} = \frac{0}{10} = 10\%$

Kitchen $\frac{20}{100} = \frac{2}{10} = 20\%$

Livingroom $\frac{25}{100} = \frac{2}{10} = 2\%$

Playroom $\frac{30}{100} = \frac{3}{10} = 30\%$

Even though they were just beginning to understand the concept of percent, it worried me that they recalled the knock-off method and used it incorrectly. Tom, who had seemed to understand fractions in December, ended up with equivalent fractions that made no sense at all a month later.

Suggested Reading

Baroody, A. J. 1989. "Manipulatives Don't Come with Guarantees." *Arithmetic Teacher* 37(2): 4–5.

Lining Up the Decimal

My combination class of seventh through twelfth grade English-as-a-Second-Language students focused on mathematical vocabulary in English and basic math concepts to assist them in content-area classes. We had been studying addition and subtraction of decimals, using money as our medium because of its familiarity to the students. We had discussed place value to the extent that 10 pennies are needed to make 1 dime and 10 dimes are needed to make 1 dollar. This concept was practiced using manipulative play money as well as transparent "coins" on the overhead projector.

Now we were ready to add and subtract decimals presented in realistic situations. First, we practiced doing word problems together so they could learn how to line up the decimals and know where to place the decimal point after adding or subtracting. The students were encouraged to use the money to help them figure out the answers to the problems. Then we set up play stores around the room, using ads cut from newspapers to show things that the students could pretend to buy. They had to find the total cost of buying several items and figure out the change using play bills and coins. We even set up a school-supply store, where students could purchase pencils, tablets, and other items with real money. Students took turns serving as shopkeepers and being responsible for the necessary computations.

After these hands-on applications, most students seemed able to line up the decimals when adding amounts of money and seemed to understand the importance of keeping the decimals in a straight line. For example, they could easily complete problems such as the one below.

$$\$5.25 + \$16 + \$0.23 + \$9.83 = ?$$

Thinking they could easily apply these skills to nonmoney numbers, I gave a problem using numbers of similar form but without the decimal signs. I reminded them to line the numbers up vertically and then add. They were asked to come to a consensus on the answer within their group. As they began to work on the problem below, Hector blurted out, "Teacher, you forgot the decimal point in the 56."

$$56 + 1.35 + 81.7 + .41 = ?$$

When I asked the students where they thought the decimal point belonged, I got back many blank stares, as well as answers ranging from "before the 5" (.56) to "between the 5 and 6" (5.6) to "after the 6" (56.). For some reason, they could identify $16 as $16.00, but didn't know where to put the decimal in 56. Why had the students' apparent mastery suddenly evaporated? Had I only taught an algorithm? I had hoped I was teaching a concept.

Suggested Reading

Borasi, R. 1990. "The Invisible Hand Operating in Mathematics Instruction: Students' Conceptions and Expectations." In *Teaching and Learning Mathematics in the 1990s,* edited by T. J. Cooney and C. R. Hirsch, 174–182. Reston, VA: The National Council of Teachers of Mathematics.

Hiebert, J. 1984. "Children's Mathematical Learning: The Struggle to Link Form and Understanding." *The Elementary School Journal* 84(5): 497–513.

Hiebert, J. 1990. "The Role of Routine Procedures in the Development of Mathematical Competence." In *Teaching and Learning Mathematics in the 1990s,* edited by T. J. Cooney and C. R. Hirsch, 31–40. Reston, VA: The National Council of Teachers of Mathematics.

Schielack, J. F. 1991. "Reaching Young Pupils with Technology." *Arithmetic Teacher* 38(6): 51–55.

A Proportion Puzzle

It was my first experience teaching pre-algebra to junior high students, and I was determined that they master the concepts of ratio and proportion. I could remember my dad saying that these were among the few things he'd learned in eighth-grade math that he'd used all his life. My students already had considerable practice solving proportions like the ones below, using an algorithm of "reduce, cross multiply, divide."

$$\frac{1}{3} = \frac{n}{15} \text{ or } \frac{2}{5} = \frac{8}{n}$$

But they were having trouble with word problems. For the homework assignment, I made up a series of relatively simple proportion problems, so that students would intuitively know whether or not their answers made sense. A typical example was the following:

A whale goes 15 miles in 45 minutes; how long will it take to go 30 miles?

I had put on the board and gone through what I thought was a reasonably clear approach to setting up proportions. First, read through the problem and look for a pair of numbers that are linked; second, turn this pair into a ratio and write it as a fraction; third, record the units (miles, ounces, etc.) for both numerator and denominator; fourth, after an equal sign, set up a second ratio, using the remaining number and n for the number you're looking for; fifth, be sure your second ratio has the same units top and bottom as the first; sixth, solve for n. The above problem would then look like this:

$$\frac{15 \text{ mi.}}{45 \text{ min.}} = \frac{30 \text{ mi.}}{n \text{ min.}}$$

Before assigning homework, I gave them a series of practice problems that we worked through together and discussed. Sam was one of several relatively good students who felt that putting down the units was just unnecessary effort, so I stopped by his desk to check his work. Just as I'd suspected, he'd set up one of his problems with the second ratio inverted. He'd "solved" what he'd set up, but his answer was way off. I asked him if it made sense: "If a bird flies 20 miles in 30 minutes (or less than 1 mile in 1 minute), would it really go over 67 miles in 45 minutes? That's a lot more than 1 mile per minute!" Sam agreed that it didn't sound right and gave it another try.

$$\frac{20}{30 \text{ min.}} = \frac{n}{45 \text{ min.}}$$

This time he got the right answer, and I didn't argue about the lack of units in the numerators. But before I could enjoy my moment of satisfaction, Chris asked: "Why are you doing it the hard way? Why don't you just turn the first 2 numbers into a decimal? I just divide the 2 by the 3 on my calculator and multiply that times 45."

Estelle argued that you didn't need any of these complications; you could just look at the 30 and 45. "Anyone can see that 45 is just 30 plus another half. So you can take the 20 plus $\frac{1}{2}$ of 20 and get the answer."

Looking back, I'm still concerned about how much to let students rely on their ability to figure out the answer to a simple problem without using an algorithm. When should I force them to use the algorithm?

Suggested Reading

Cramer, K., and T. Post. 1993. "Making Connections: A Case for Proportionality." *Arithmetic Teacher* 40(6): 342–346.

Curcio, F. R. 1990. "Mathematics as Communication: Using a Language-Experience Approach in the Elementary Grades." In *Teaching and Learning Mathematics in the 1990s*, edited by T. J. Cooney and C. R. Hirsch, 69–75. Reston, VA: The National Council of Teachers of Mathematics.

Teaching as Questioning

The only way in which a human being can make some approach to knowing the whole of a subject is by hearing what can be said about it by persons of every variety of opinion, and studying all modes in which it can be looked at by every character of mind. No wise man ever acquired his wisdom in any other manner.

JOHN STUART MILL

Zeros Sometimes Make a Difference

Students have been taught that when you multiply or divide whole numbers by powers of 10, all you have to do is add or remove zeros. In reality this is a misteaching, a simplification of the fact that the digits of the chosen number shift place-value columns. One could say that it is the decimal point which moves and that this sometimes requires the addition of a zero as a place holder or the removal of an existing but unnecessary zero.

When students enter fifth grade and the world of decimal fractions, this strategy fails them. One cannot make .17 bigger by adding two zeros, for that will result in .1700, an equivalent decimal. Conversely, one cannot make .40 ten times smaller (divide by 10) by removing one zero, for that will result in .4—again an equivalent decimal.

As a teacher for 15 years, I have found that place-value confusions permeate the decimal work of fifth and sixth graders. Most become competent at algorithms but often flounder with subsequent units because of their underlying misunderstandings. The most successful remedies I have found lie in the use of manipulatives and of small group discussions to help develop understanding. I base decisions about group composition on students' objective computational ability and on my subjective assessment of each one's mathematical thinking ability.

I teach a combined fifth and sixth grade class in a small, progressive private elementary school. As a school we take pride in our commitment to multiethnic classrooms with children of varying academic abilities and potential. Teacher-student relationships become strong and personal, allowing for intimate discussion of student work without embarrassment or anxiety.

Ever since I moved beyond ordering and comparing decimals using decimal place-value squares, a manipulative, Woody had been lost. In our small groups I would notice him looking confused and distracted. Although I could always pull him back into the discussion, I knew he and I were overdue for a conference.

When Woody came to meet with me, I told him I had noticed his confusion when we were comparing decimals. I expressed my interest in understanding what he was thinking about.

I asked him to work on some problems with me. Assuming this was not an anxiety-producing situation, I began with some fairly difficult decimal comparisons.

I wrote down .47 and .04 and asked him which was greater. He explained that .47 was bigger because each number had been broken into little bits and one had 47 of them. Then I wrote down .17 and .047 and asked him to compare these. He explained that .047 was bigger because it has 47 little pieces where .17 only has 17 little pieces. Woody continued by saying, "Zero is nothing, so it doesn't make a difference." I then wrote down .17 and .170, and he knew they were the same, explaining again that "you can add zeros to a number because they are nothing." Probing deeper, I wrote .017 and .17. He said that these too were the same and that .00047 was greater than .17 "because you can add zeros to a number without changing it."

Thinking a concrete analogy would help Woody better understand, I asked him to think about money. Writing .04 and .17, I asked which was greater. He knew that .17 was more. Adding a 7 to the thousandths column of .04, I then asked him to compare .047 and .17. He said .047 was more. "But if zero is nothing," I asked, "how could adding this 7 make .047 greater than .17?" Woody looked puzzled. Trying to accommodate this new information, he now stated, "The zero sometimes changes things."

We looked at a few more examples. He said that .47 was equal to .470 and .47 to .047. But when I covered up the 7 in .047, the .47 became much bigger.

Pushing further, I wrote: .1; .10; .01; and 1.00. Then I asked, "Thinking about money, what would you call these decimals?" After he answered correctly, I said, "But if zero is nothing and doesn't make a difference, why aren't these numbers the same?" Again, looking puzzled, he said, "For some reason the zero sometimes does make a difference."

We concluded the session with my saying that "sometimes a zero makes a difference and sometimes it doesn't." I told him we would work together to sort out when these times were.

After school that day, I looked back on my notes and tried to decide how to proceed. I could teach him another algorithm, in which the decimal point serves as an anchor and zeros on the peripheries are dispensable. But what would really help him to better understand place value?

I also wondered how he would have responded if I had asked him to compare .5 and .4? Did he have any sense of the relative magnitude of the fractional pieces?

Suggested Reading

Cuevas, G. 1990. "Increasing the Achievement and Participation of Language Minority Students in Mathematics Education." In *Teaching and Learning Mathematics in the 1990s*, edited by T. J. Cooney and C. R. Hirsch, 159–165. Reston, VA: The National Council of Teachers of Mathematics.

Long, M. J., and M. Ben-Hur. 1991. "Informing Learning Through the Clinical Interview." *Arithmetic Teacher* 38(6): 44–46.

Webb, N., and D. Briars. 1990. "Assessment in Mathematics Classrooms, K–8." In *Teaching and Learning Mathematics in the 1990s*, edited by T. J. Cooney and C. R. Hirsch, 108–117. Reston, VA: The National Council of Teachers of Mathematics.

Six-Tenths or Four-Fifths of a Dollar?

The math experiences of the 30 students in my fourth-grade class vary widely. Esmarelda, a recent immigrant to the United States, is Limited English Proficient (LEP) and has never had formal schooling. Chris is a gifted student who enjoys calculations and problem solving. Michael participates in my class, then later in the day goes to the resource room for additional math help. There are also 3 children with special needs, 4 other LEP students, and 12 extremely economically disadvantaged students.

Often, it seems, I teach a lesson 4 or 5 times before I feel comfortable moving ahead. Sometimes I worry that I'm beating a dead horse. For those students who catch on quickly I try to plan enrichment activities or set up activity centers. This year—my third year of teaching—I've been trying to include more math journal writing before, during, and after lessons. I also try to use concrete materials before explaining a mathematical concept to the class.

I recently introduced the class to fractions. They have learned how to identify fractions using diagrams such as the following:

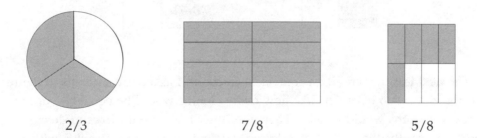

| 2/3 | 7/8 | 5/8 |

Each student made a fraction kit that allowed them to show and identify various fractions. The denominators of the fractions in the kits were 1, 2, 4, 8, and 16.

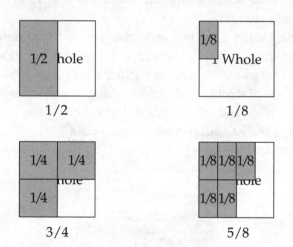

| 1/8 | 1/8 | 1/8 | 1/8 |

| 1/16 | 1/16 | 1/16 | 1/16 |

My beginning lesson had focused on identifying and orally naming various fractions.

"Place your 'whole' on the desk top," I said. "Show me $\frac{1}{4}$ of a whole by placing $\frac{1}{4}$ on top of it." The students responded by placing a "one-fourth" piece on the square representing 1 whole.

By the end of the lesson, they could successfully name and use the fraction kit to show unit fractions like $\frac{1}{2}$ or $\frac{1}{8}$ and nonunit fractions like $\frac{3}{4}$ or $\frac{5}{8}$.

1/2   1/8   3/4   5/8

The next lesson focused on equivalent fractions. I asked the students to figure out the answer to questions like how many eighths would be equal to $\frac{1}{4}$ or how many sixteenths would equal $\frac{3}{8}$. They used their fraction-kit pieces to determine the answers. By the end of this lesson, students were very familiar with the relationship among the fraction pieces and could solve simple equivalency problems without using the pieces.

I was then ready to have students learn how to compare fractions that have different denominators and numerators. Prior to beginning, I asked them to write about fraction equivalency in their journals, so I could assess their understanding of previous lessons and know what information I needed to cover. I asked them to answer this question:

Which would you rather have: $\frac{6}{10}$ of a dollar or $\frac{4}{5}$ of a dollar? Explain your reasons for choosing your answer.

After reflecting, the students picked up their pencils and wrote.

Cindy's journal read: "If I had $\frac{6}{10}$, I would have 2 more than $\frac{4}{5}$. I would choose $\frac{6}{10}$ so I could have more money."

Chris wrote: "$\frac{4}{5} = \frac{8}{10}$. $\frac{8}{10}$ is greater than $\frac{6}{10}$. Of course, I'd take $\frac{4}{5}$ of a dollar. Wouldn't you?" He included an illustration:

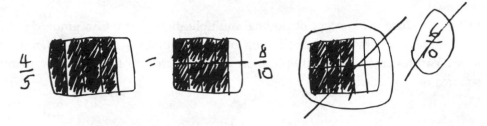

Esmarelda wrote: "No sé. $\frac{6}{10}$ es mas grande."

Nikki drew a picture to accompany her answer: "I want $\frac{6}{10}$. It is bigger."

Only 4 of the 30 students wrote $\frac{4}{5}$. Their journals gave me some hints about how they were thinking about fractions, but I was not sure how to use this information to plan our future work. Since the students were familiar with the fraction kit, I wondered if they would have answered differently if the question had been, "Would you rather have $\frac{3}{4}$ or $\frac{5}{8}$ of a chocolate bar?"

Suggested Reading

Behr, M. J., T. R. Post, and I. Wachsmuth. 1986. "Estimation and Children's Concept of Rational Number Size." In *Estimation and Mental Computation*, edited by H. L. Schoen and M. J. Zweng, 103–111. Reston, VA: The National Council of Teachers of Mathematics.

Cuevas, G. 1990. "Increasing the Achievement and Participation of Language Minority Students in Mathematics Education." In *Teaching and Learning Mathematics in the 1990s*, edited by T. J. Cooney and C. R. Hirsch, 159–165. Reston, VA: The National Council of Teachers of Mathematics.

Testing Theories

To introduce the concept of decimal multiplication to my fifth grade class, I began by reviewing multiplication of whole numbers using a rectangular array. We discussed why multiplication could be used to find out how many squares were in the array.

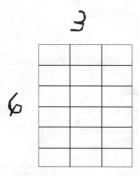

After this 5 minute review, I said that today we would see how this same idea could be applied to multiplying decimals. On the overhead projector, I showed 2 large squares, 1 directly above the other, each divided into 100 small squares. Then I shaded in a block that was 12 small squares up and 5 small squares across.

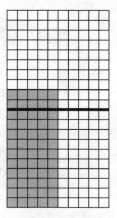

I pointed out that there were 100 small squares in each large square and asked how many small squares were shaded.

"Sixty," several children responded immediately.

"Yes. Now let's think how these numbers, 12 and 5, could be represented in terms of decimals. There are 5 squares across out of 10, aren't there? How could we say '5 out of 10' as a decimal?"

They thought for a moment and Gil said, "5 tenths?"

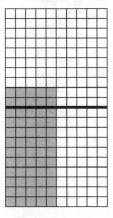

.5

I wrote "$\frac{5}{10}$ = .5" on the board and reminded them that we had followed this process when we first looked at the meaning of decimals. "Now," I continued, "how can we write the 12 squares going up as a decimal?" They frowned, and I prompted: "It takes 10 to make 1 complete side, doesn't it? And we have 12, so how could we write that?"

"Maybe it's 1.2," said Derrick, "because it's 1 whole square and $\frac{2}{10}$ more of another square."

"Exactly!" I wrote "$1\frac{2}{10}$ = 1.2" on the board.

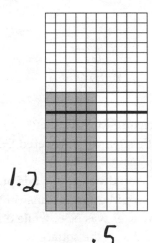

1.2

.5

"Now that means our multiplication problem is really 1.2 × .5, doesn't it? So I wonder, then, if we need a decimal point in our answer? We don't have 60 large squares, we have 60 little ones. In fact, those 60 little squares don't even make up one large square, do they? So how could we express the 60 little squares as a decimal?"

"Sixty hundredths?" Nicky said, a little tentatively. When I asked why, the class agreed that it was because we had 60 squares out of 100.

I wrote "$\frac{60}{100} = .60$" on the board. Then I wrote:

$$\begin{array}{r} 1.2 \\ \times\ \ .5 \\ \hline .60 \end{array}$$

Together we drew diagrams of several similar problems, and then they drew a few independently in their notebooks. When they finished, I wrote the problems and their answers on the board and asked if they could see any pattern to the placement of the decimal point in the answers.

$$\begin{array}{cccccccc} 1.2 & 2.2 & 1.8 & .7 & 2.8 & 2.4 & 1.5 & .9 \\ \times\ .4 & \times\ .6 & \times\ .5 & \times.6 & .4 & \times\ .2 & .3 & \times.4 \\ \hline .48 & 1.32 & .90 & .42 & 1.12 & .48 & .45 & .36 \end{array}$$

"You always count over 2 places," said Jeff.

Nicky said, "Whenever you are multiplying the last digits together and you have to carry, you put the number you carried on the left of the decimal."

"I think you count how many numbers are to the right of the decimal in each one and then do that many in the answer," Shirlyn offered.

"We have three theories that all seem to fit," I said. "Let's test them some more. If I wrote—

$$\begin{array}{r} 6.7 \\ \times .08 \end{array}$$

—How would you draw a picture to work this?"

"You'd have to have 1000 little squares," answered Derrick without hesitation. I was surprised at his certainty.

"Yes, you would," I agreed. "Would you all try this problem and see if you can guess where the decimal point would go in the answer?"

Some students thought the answer was 5.36, while others thought it was .536. I reminded them that Derrick had said the square would have to be divided into 1,000 small squares and asked if 536 of these very small squares would give them 5 whole squares. After a little more discussion, I think most of them were convinced that the answer had to be .536. I now asked how the three theories had held up on this problem.

"Mine doesn't work," Jeff admitted. Like several of my students, Jeff has come a long way this year. He is more willing to take risks and realizes that his classmates are expected to be supportive even when his theory doesn't work out.

"Shirlyn's has to be right," Nicky said, as she flipped the page in her math book. "Hey, she *is* right. Look, it's right here on the next page under 'Short Cut'!"

I encouraged Nicky to push a little more deeply into her own theory to see if it too might explain this.

Suggested Reading

Damarin, S. K. 1990. "Teaching Mathematics: A Feminist Perspective." In *Teaching and Learning Mathematics in the 1990s*, edited by T. J. Cooney and C. R. Hirsch, 144–151. Reston, VA: The National Council of Teachers of Mathematics.

Hiebert, J. 1992. "Mathematical, Cognitive, and Instructional Analyses of Decimal Fractions." In *Analysis of Arithmetic for Mathematics Teaching*, edited by G. Leinhardt, R. Putnam, and R. A. Hattrup, 283–322. Hillsdale, NJ: Lawrence Erlbaum Associates.

Stigler, J. W. 1988. "Research into Practice: The Use of Verbal Explanation in Japanese and American Classrooms." *Arithmetic Teacher* 36(2): 27–29.

Stigler, J. W., and H. W. Stevenson. 1991. "How Asian Teachers Polish Each Lesson to Perfection." *American Educator* 15(1): 12–47.

Webb, N., and D. Briars. 1990. "Assessment in Mathematics Classrooms, K–8." In *Teaching and Learning Mathematics in the 1990s*, edited by T. J. Cooney and C. R. Hirsch, 108–117. Reston, VA: The National Council of Teachers of Mathematics.

Hugh's Invention

Everyone seemed involved in our math investigation today. They were measuring their giant steps, hops, standing jumps, smiles, and anything else that interested them. They performed, measured, and then performed and measured again, so that they could compare measures and decide when they had reached their maximum performance. They were using a collection of materials to measure: straws, toothpicks, interlocking cubes, paper clips, coffee stirrers, and measuring tapes.

I was especially interested to see how they would communicate measures that were not exact—the case arising in almost every instance. (This investigation precludes any formal focus on fractions.) What language would they use verbally? How would they articulate the language in print? Would they ask for advice? Would they talk among themselves? I was also interested to see which materials they chose. Would they choose longer units for longer measures and shorter ones for shorter measures? Would they understand that they had to use the same measure if they wanted to compare one giant jump to another? Would they start to make the connection that there is a relationship between the size of the unit and the number of units it takes to measure an object?

I roved and observed. They were motivated to beat their measures and excited when they did. In my wanderings, I happened to glance at Hugh's recording sheet. I was intrigued. He had recorded his giant step as $130\frac{29}{31}$ cm. I needed to talk to Hugh.

Me:	Hugh, how's it going?
Hugh:	Good! I'm going to beat my giant step. I know it. Wanna watch?
Me:	Sure. How long was your last one?
Hugh:	*(Referring to his record)* $130\frac{29}{31}$ cm.
Me:	*(Pointing to the fraction)* Tell me about this here. What does it mean?
Hugh:	Well I almost jumped 131 cm, so I wrote it that way. It means I was really close.

I still needed to know more. It wasn't a fraction that I expected to see, but Hugh was impatient. Everything seemed obvious to him and he wanted to get on with breaking his record. I decided to leave him to it and returned to the conversation later when the activity was over.

Me: You know Hugh, I've been thinking about what you told me about your jumping. I'd like you to explain why you chose $\frac{29}{31}$.

Hugh: I just did. *(Long pause)* You know, you can choose anything you want.

Me: What do you mean, "Anything you want"?

Hugh: Well, you do. You just choose—it could be 31 or 15 or 78 or anything you want.

Me: What if you had chosen 78?

Hugh: Well, then I wouldn't have 29, I'd have 72. No, probably 74.

Me: And if you had chosen 15?

Hugh: Probably 13 or 14 . . . 'cause it was close to the next one.

Me: The next one?

Hugh: *(Sounding impatient with me)* Yeah, to 131.

I still needed to talk, and I could tell that Hugh was ready for the conversation to end. I decided to introduce another model and hope he would stick it out so that I could probe a bit more. A perfect question popped into mind.

Me: So you say that the number can be anything. I understand. Here's a straw and I'm putting my thumb against it. What if I decide that the straw is 20. How long would you say my thumb is?

Hugh: *(Taking a look)* Well, your thumb isn't 15. So it's 5. Yeah, $\frac{5}{20}$.

I still couldn't let go. I was more and more intrigued and distracted by Hugh's thinking.

Me: You say that the straw can be anything, and I think I understand. But I'm wondering, can it be anything? Is there a number that wouldn't work to describe the length of my thumb?

Hugh: *(Responding in a flash)* It couldn't be a third . . . no, not a third. 'Cause it's smaller . . . No, I couldn't use thirds. *(A long pause—for some reason which I didn't question. I could see he was still thinking about that. A huge smile appeared across his face)* Oh wait! I could do it in thirds. It's about as long as $\frac{3}{4}$ of a $\frac{1}{3}$ of the straw. *(A short pause)* So I can use thirds.

The conversation ended because Hugh's explanation left me speechless. I was so aware that he had only just celebrated his seventh birthday.

I began the investigation looking for how children communicated their discoveries and how they engaged in a measurement task. I was quickly distracted by Hugh as our conversation began.

I began the conversation intrigued and left it even more so. Hugh behaves just like the other seven-year-olds, and in many ways I would describe him as young for his age.

What experiences have helped him reason about proportions at the early age of seven? What other mathematical ideas has he grasped in such a sophisticated form?

If these ideas are accessible to Hugh, are there other children in the class that also have developed such insights—made such powerful connections?

Suggested Reading

Carter, H. L. 1986. "Linking Estimation to Psychological Variables in the Early Years." In *Estimation and Mental Computation,* edited by H. L. Schoen and M. J. Zweng, 74–81. Reston, VA: The National Council of Teachers of Mathematics.

Kamii, C. 1990. "Constructivism and Beginning Arithmetic K–12." In *Teaching and Learning Mathematics in the 1990s,* edited by T. J. Cooney and C. R. Hirsch, 22–30. Reston, VA: The National Council of Teachers of Mathematics.

Thirteen Can't Fit Over Twelve

$\textbf{M}$y seventh graders bustled in for the last class before lunch and quickly found a seat. Most students opened their notebooks to last night's homework. I began reading the problems and answers at a rapid pace so students could check their own homework. At one point, I noticed Craig looking disappointed.

"What's wrong?" I asked. He told me he got number 27 wrong.

"What did you get?"

"Forty-eight and $\frac{13}{12}$," he replied in a barely audible voice.

After I asked him to repeat his answer, he said, "Oh, I see now."

"What do you see, Craig?"

"Thirteen can't fit over 12."

"Sure it can," I said as I went to the chalkboard and "fit" 13 over 12.

This response may seem flippant, but I wanted to make the point that the precise nature of mathematical definitions cannot be overemphasized. Although my students occasionally groan at my insistence, they don't miss my point.

"I mean, it's not supposed to," said Craig.

"What do you mean 'it's not supposed to?' Be more explicit."

"It's improper," he finally offered.

"What has to be true for it to be *improper*?" I asked, looking to the whole class for an answer.

"The top has to be smaller than the bottom," Raisa ventured.

"Raise your hand if you agree with that statement," I said, looking around the room. "Helen doesn't agree. Jack doesn't agree."

I asked Mary to repeat Raisa's statement, while I wrote the following on the board:

$$\underline{\text{Improper fraction}} \quad n > d$$

Instead of telling the students the answer, I subject statements to their collective scrutiny and allow the class to continue struggling to arrive at an acceptable definition.

"I disagree because the numerator is the bottom number and the denominator is the top number," Kia stated. Ameenah shook her head in disagreement.

"Kia, Ameenah thinks you're wrong," I said, interpreting her gesture. "How could you figure out who is right and who is wrong?"

"Look it up!" shouted one student in the front of the class.

"How else?"

"Ask somebody!" another student suggested, giggling.

"Anyone have a different way?"

Finally, Dimarco recalled a class discussion some time ago about how to remember which part of the fraction is the numerator and which is the denominator. "Numerator has the word number in it," he said. "Since the top tells how many, it has to be on top."

This triggered another student's memory that denominator is like denomination, it tells which church group.

"Yes, it separates into groups." I agreed. "Denominator tells what kind of piece it is." I wrote $\frac{1}{4}$ on the board and asked, "What kind of piece is this?"

"A fourth," the whole class answered.

"That's right. So Stacy, an improper fraction is when . . ." I paused, waiting for Stacy to complete the sentence.

"The numerator is bigger than the denominator," Stacy replied.

Everyone nodded enthusiastically.

"Okay," I said, "raise your right hand if the fraction I write on the board is improper and raise your left if the fraction is proper." I made certain everyone understood which hand was for what and then wrote the first fraction on the board.

$$\frac{7}{8}$$

"I see left hands up. So it's proper. Is that correct?" All the students nodded their heads in agreement. Then I wrote another fraction on the board.

$$\frac{9}{8}$$

"Right hands, right hands, everybody thinks it's an . . ."

"Improper fraction!" they shouted enthusiastically.

It would have been easy for me to leave it at this—the students had demonstrated their ability to apply their definition to various fractions. However, I wanted them to stretch their understanding, to apply it to an exotic yet accessible problem.

So I wrote the following complex fraction on the board. The students couldn't decide how to respond.

$$\frac{\frac{1}{3}}{\frac{2}{3}}$$

"I see left hands . . . I see shrugs . . . I see both hands," I reported as I surveyed the room.

"This is called a complex fraction," I explained. "What's on top?"

The class responded "One-third."

"What's on bottom?"

The class responded "Two-thirds."

"Which is bigger, the numerator or the denominator?" They all agreed that the denominator was larger and the fraction was proper.

Thinking the surprises were over, the students were baffled once again when I wrote the following fraction on the board.

$$\frac{9}{9}$$

"I don't want to see two hands," I told them. "Commit yourselves. Who thinks it's proper, raise your hands. Improper?" I waited, giving students time to grapple with the question. Finally, the hands showed that the class was divided.

"It's not proper," I began. "What kind of number is it?"

"It's a whole number," several students finally responded.

By this time half the class period had already passed. Feeling a little pressed for time, I told them, "If the numerator is the *same* or bigger than the denominator then it's improper." Then I pointed to the "$n > d$" inequality on the board and asked who could read it.

"n is greater than d," one student read. Then I wrote $n \geq d$ on the board and asked the class to read it.

"n is greater than or equal to d," they read.

"This defines an improper fraction. Nine-ninths is improper. Why? By definition," I said. I then turned the class's attention back to Craig's problem, which he had written on the board.

$$48\frac{13}{12}$$

"What is the correct way to write the improper fraction $\frac{13}{12}$? How much more or less is it than 1?" I looked to Craig for an answer.

"I don't know," he said.

"Twelve-twelfths is 1, so how much more than that is this number?" I asked.

"One-twelfth," Craig answered. I wrote $1\frac{1}{12}$ on the board under the $\frac{13}{12}$ and said, "Now explain what the answer will be, Craig."

Craig completed the transformation, "You add one more whole to 48 to make 49. It's 49 and $\frac{1}{12}$."

Epilogue

I hope to do an excellent job teaching mathematical concepts and skills, but there is something equally significant I hope to accomplish—getting children to think for themselves. I want them to know that they are the only ones who can decide what they know and what they believe, that they must be the ones to construct their own meaning and reality. My ultimate goal is to help students develop a disposition toward critical thinking.

In this case, correcting homework is the forum for helping students better understand the defining characteristics of improper and proper fractions. To some degree, the process the students went through here modeled the way a mathematical definition might develop. First, a general meaning is stated, then, as possible exceptions arise, the definition is adjusted to include or exclude. Finally, a conclusive, clear, and precise definition is attained. This is especially important in mathematics, since subsequent axioms and theorems are built on these definitions.

I could have handed the students the definition for proper and improper fractions, asked them to memorize it, and then tested them to see if they could apply it. But no thinking—critical or otherwise—would have taken place.

Instead, I expose my students to a discussion that bounces back and forth, asking them to agree or disagree with statements made by their peers. I try to avoid saying who is right or wrong. Rather, I subject all statements to class scrutiny. I point out when there is agreement and when there isn't, and I let the students correct each other.

Some teachers believe it is their task to make things clear and simple for their students. An opposing view is presented by John Passmore in his article, "On Teaching to Be Critical," where he writes that one of the educator's tasks is to "make his students puzzled." So when things were going along smoothly, I injected something new—the complex fraction. With some gentle nudging, my students were able to distinguish the numerator from the denominator and determine that the fraction in question was proper. Then I puzzled them again by presenting a fraction in which the numerator and denominator were equal, forcing them to further refine their evolving definition.

I agree with Barry Beyer, who writes about the teaching of thinking skills:

> *Classrooms that welcome student thinking provide the reinforcement and*
> *support that encourage students to 'risk' thinking. Such classrooms help*

students feel free to challenge, question, invent, and guess. Information processing, rather than information receiving, is the major activity.

Suggested Reading

Beyer, B. 1983. "Common Sense About Teaching Skills." *Educational Leadership* 41(3): 44–49.

Borasi, R. 1990. "The Invisible Hand Operating in Mathematics Instruction: Students' Conceptions and Expectations." In *Teaching and Learning Mathematics in the 1990s,* edited by T. J. Cooney and C. R. Hirsch, 174–182. Reston, VA: The National Council of Teachers of Mathematics.

Passmore, J. 1967. "On Teaching to Be Critical." In *The Concept of Education,* edited by R. S. Peters. London: Routledge & Kegan Paul.

SOME OF THE INSTRU
MATERIALS USED I
CLASSROOM
WERE PERSONALLY PU
BY THE
TEACHER

I N S T

Reflecting

Never doubt that a small group of thoughtful,
committed people can change the world.
Indeed, it's the only thing that ever has.

MARGARET MEAD

Problem of the Week: "Bounce, Bounce"

Among my thirty sixth-grade students there is a lot of variation in ability level. According to their California Test of Basic Skills scores, their ability levels range from the second grade to the tenth grade. Several are gifted students who always welcome new, difficult challenges in problem solving. One student has recently qualified for the Resource Specialist Program and receives special help in math and language arts three days a week. Another student is a non-English speaker. In addition, my class has four resource students, eight Gifted And Talented Education (GATE) students, and four Limited English Proficient students.

In an effort to expand the students' writing experience in mathematics, I assign a "Problem of the Week" (also known as "POW"). In their written responses, students must first restate the problem (2 points); second, describe the problem-solving process or processes used, including strategies and thinking (3 points); third, discuss any learning that took place (3 points); and fourth, present and analyze their solution or solutions (2 points).

During math on Monday, the POW is presented. By Wednesday, students are ready to give hints to others who are stuck, suggesting possible strategies. Then, before turning in their POW write-ups on Friday, students share with one another.

Since the beginning of the school year, I have seen tremendous growth in students' ability to express their thinking and learning through writing. This growth can be attributed first to the fact that each week, in pairs or in groups, students share with the whole class different ways of solving the same problem. Thus, they learn from each other. Second, as a class we compare and discuss anonymous papers. By mid-year students were evaluating peers' papers according to the rubric. Third, some POWs are assigned as an in-class small group task with students working cooperatively on one write-up. Finally, the grading emphasis is on the process of problem solving and a student's ability to communicate clearly and concisely his or her thinking, not simply on coming up with the right answer. This has gradually built up students' confidence levels.

Here is the POW we did this week:

"Bounce, Bounce"
If a ball is dropped from the top of a 64 foot building and it bounces exactly half the height from which it is dropped, how high will the ball bounce on its eighth bounce?

Despite the considerable diversity in the class, as usual almost all the students were able to work through the problem. Step one presented no problem, and for step two, most students used either a picture/diagram or a function table—usually carefully labeled—to represent and help solve the problem. In step three, many students confidently stated the problem was "just right" or "simple" and then proceeded to explain their thinking in step 4.

Students used one of four mathematical approaches to solve the problem: dividing, subtracting, adding, and "taking half." Regardless of the chosen strategy, they discovered a consistent pattern and completed it successfully—up to the sixth bounce. At this point their thinking began to diverge, and, depending on the mathematical approach used, several error patterns emerged.

Many of the students who interpreted the problem as a subtraction one ($64 - 32 = 32$; $32 - 16 = 16$; $16 - 8 = 8$; $8 - 4 = 4$; and so on) did fine until they got to 1. At this point, several students were stuck and said the answer must be zero. Derrick managed to subtract $\frac{1}{2}$ from 1 but still got zero by subtracting $\frac{1}{2}$ from $\frac{1}{2}$, instead of subtracting $\frac{1}{4}$ from $\frac{1}{2}$ to get $\frac{1}{4}$. His work is shown.

Derrick's work

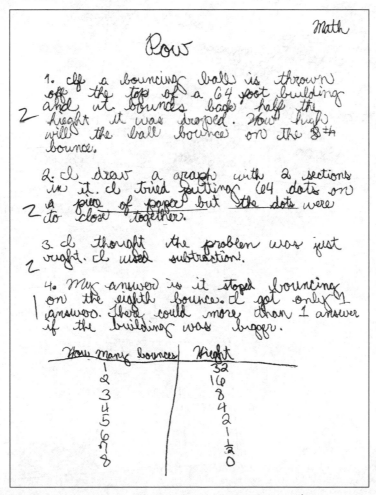

The students using division (64 ÷ 2 = 32; 32 ÷ 2 = 16; 16 ÷ 2 = 8; and so on) ran into difficulty when they had to divide 1 by 2. They arrived at "no bounce" for an answer. Leslie was one of these.

Leslie's work

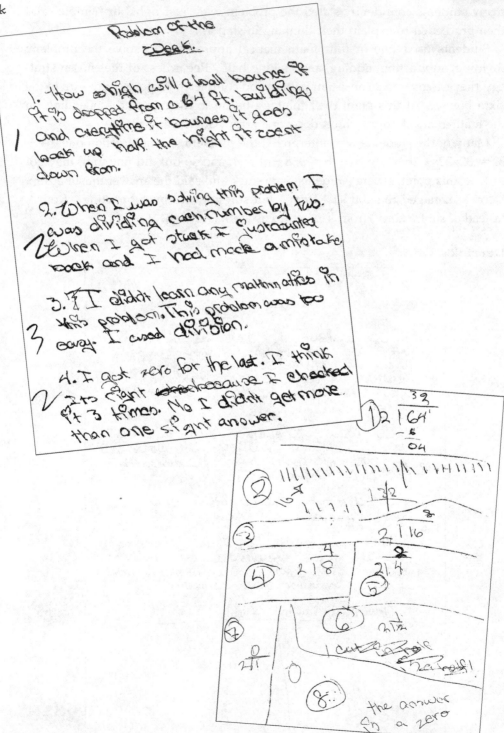

Students who "*took* half" each time gave an answer of $\frac{1}{4}$ foot or 3 inches, which was the correct response. Donald and Jennifer were among the few who actually got all ten points on this problem.

Donald's work

1. If you drop a ball off of a 64 foot building and on its first bounce it bounces exactly half of the height from which it is dropped from. How high will the ball bounce if it is on its eighth bounce?

2. What I done in trying to solve this problem was first I put 64 and said half of 64 is 32. Then I done the same thing to all of the bounces. The answer I got was 1/4.

64 = 32	1	Bounce
32 = 16	2	Bounce
16 = 8	3	Bounce
8 = 4	4	Bounce
4 = 2	5	Bounce
2 = 1 ft	6	Bounce
1 = 1/2	7	Bounce
1/2 = (1/4)	8	Bounce

Thats what I tried. That worked. I don't know what didn't work because I only did one way. I never got stuck. I used a table method for mathematics. I didn't learn anything about myself. I think the problem was too easy.

4. The answer I got was 1/4. I think its right because I work out the problem. I only got one right answer. I don't know if there could be another answer

Jennifer's work

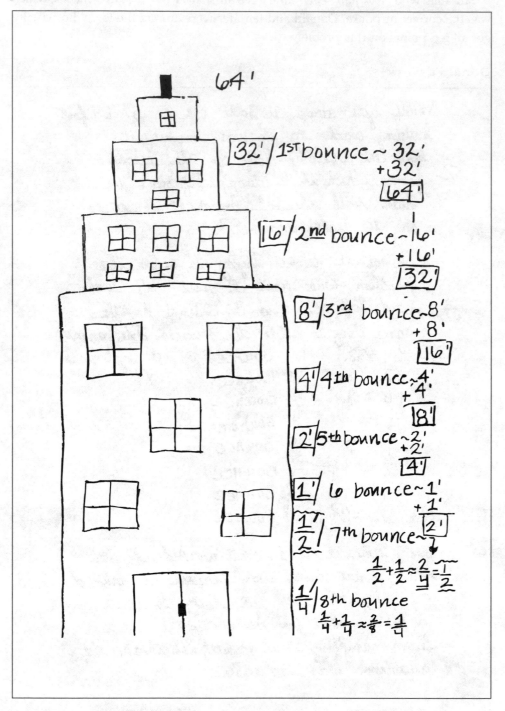

Although their strategies had worked up to a point, many students did not, or were unable to, question the validity of their answers, asking "Does this make sense?" Of course it made sense to them, because they had followed through with their strategy.

I wondered how to motivate students like Aaron. Last week, Aaron was the only one to interpret the POW correctly and thus come up with a reasonable solution. This week, however, his response was the following: "I didn't ask anybody for help 'cause I did it at night. I didn't use any mathematics 'cause I didn't get a mathematical answer. The problem was kind of hard. For the answer of my POW I got, 'What if the ball bounced on a nail and it popped? Then there would be no other bounce.'" I was a little disappointed that the positive reinforcement he received for solving last week's problem hadn't motivated him to give it a try this week. Aaron is a very passive learner, a low achiever in all academic areas. School seems unimportant to him, and his main goal in life is to be a professional baseball player.

Aaron's work

Pow

1. If a ball bounces if a ball is dropped from the top of a sixty four building and it bounces exactly half the height from what it is dropped, how high will the ball bounce on its eight bounce?

2. I didn't ask any body for help cause I did it at night. I didn't use any mathmatics cause I didn't get a mathematic answer.

3. The problem was kind of hard! Yes I checked and only got one answer.

4. For the answer of my pow is what if the ball bounced on a nail and poped and it will be no other bounce.

I also wrestle with several other unresolved student- and teacher-related issues. Is this a positive or negative experience for students who don't like writing or for whom writing is difficult? Is there an easier way to evaluate POWs on a weekly basis? What if I don't evaluate at all?

Suggested Reading

Holmes, E. E. 1990. "Motivation: An Essential Component of Mathematics Instruction." In *Teaching and Learning Mathematics in the 1990s,* edited by T. J. Cooney and C. R. Hirsch, 101–107. Reston, VA: The National Council of Teachers of Mathematics.

Webb, N., and D. Briars. 1990. "Assessment in Mathematics Classrooms, K–8." In *Teaching and Learning Mathematics in the 1990s,* edited by T. J. Cooney and C. R. Hirsch, 108–117. Reston, VA: The National Council of Teachers of Mathematics.

Function Machine

How in the world do I begin to introduce ratios to a class of twenty-five fourth graders? How can I teach and verify their understanding of ratios? How much additional help should be given to resource students, Limited English Proficient (LEP), and gifted students? Each time I prepare a math lesson, these same questions linger.

My goal with this particular lesson was to have the students recognize a pattern of ratios and be able to organize the information in a table. To introduce the lesson, I provided a box with a question mark written on the front.

"Does anyone know what this is?" I asked.

A surprise box, a guessing game, an "I-don't-know" box, a question box—these were some of the responses.

"Those were good guesses," I said. "I call this a Function Machine. What's a Function Machine? I'm not going to tell you; I'm going to show you what it does." I showed the class a paper with "1 person" written on it. I put the paper into the Function Machine and pulled another piece of paper from the box with "2 shoes" written on it.

"Oh, I know how it goes!" cried one of the students, as I began to draw a table on the board.

"What went into the machine?" I asked the class.

"One."

"What came out?"

"Two."

I recorded this information in the table.

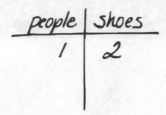

Showing them a paper with "2 people" written on it, I asked, "Can anyone guess what will come out?" Lots of hands were raised.

Among the responses were: "One shoe," "I know Ms. Mendes!" "So do I!" "Four shoes," "Three shoes." I then put in the paper and pulled out another with "4 shoes" written on it and recorded this on the table.

people	shoes
1	2
2	4

"Do you have predictions about what will come next?" I asked.

"Three people; 8 shoes, no, 6 shoes," some students replied.

"Can anyone explain the pattern here?"

"You have 1, 2, 3, 4," Sandy answered.

"Two, 4, 6, 8," Derek added.

I then asked the students to pull out their math journals. I asked them to copy the table, write about the patterns they saw, and predict what they thought would come out if we put "3 people" in the machine.

Walking around the room to observe students, I noticed that Tom and Sandy were using pictures to illustrate the table. Tom loves math, easily completes assignments and loves to embellish his work with illustrations. Sandy thinks math is "okay" but avoids using numbers to solve problems. Sandy's pictorial representation of the problem looked like this:

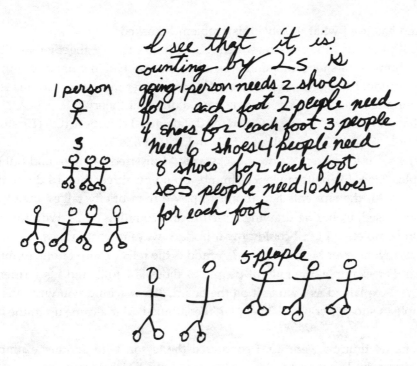

I see that it is counting by 2s is going 1 person needs 2 shoes for each foot 2 people need 4 shoes for each foot 3 people need 6 shoes 4 people need 8 shoes for each foot so 5 people need 10 shoes for each foot

1 person

3

5 people

I brought the class back together to discuss their patterns and predictions. "Now let's put '3 people' into the Function Machine. What do you think will happen?"

"Six," they responded in chorus.

people	shoes
1	2
2	4
3	6

"Does anyone have a theory about why it's 6?" I asked.

"I figured out how many people, then did 'times 2,'" Julio volunteered. I asked him to share his idea with the class. He wrote the following on the board and explained his thinking.

$$1 \times 2 = 2$$
$$2 \times 2 = 4$$
$$3 \times 2 = 6$$

"Julio has used what to solve this problem?" I asked.

"Multiplication," the class answered. Using Julio's theory, together we figured out the number of shoes for 4 and 5 people. Since we had just finished a unit on multiplication, I was pleased they were able to transfer the concept to this lesson.

Moving on, I asked, "Does anyone have a different theory?"

"I have a pattern," Sam, a Gifted And Talented Education (GATE) student, called out. "Half of 2 is 1, half of 4 is 2, and half of 6 is 3."

"Let's see if it works; let's do it backwards." I inserted 14 shoes and out came 7 people. "Does his pattern work? Thumbs up if you agree, thumbs down if you disagree." All the students had thumbs up. We then briefly talked about other strategies used, including drawing a picture and counting by 2s. With this introduction completed, I felt I could now introduce ways to write ratios.

"Has anyone ever heard of ratios? A ratio is the relationship of one number to another. For example, the ratio of people to shoes is 1 to 2, and it's written like this, $\frac{1}{2}$,'" I explained as I wrote it on the board. "How would you write the ratio of people to shoes if you had 2 people?" I continued. Maria came up to the board and wrote "$\frac{2}{4}$."

Again, all thumbs were up. I continued the lesson with another example of ratios using the Function Machine. This time I used nickels to quarters, starting with 5 nickels and 1 quarter.

nickels	quarters
5	1
10	2
15	3

After working through part of this problem, I asked my students to continue the pattern in their journals. Although Thomas saw a pattern in each column of the table, he apparently didn't see the functional relationship between the corresponding numbers in each column. Several students were still at a similar level of understanding.

Nickles | Quarters
5 | 1
10 | 2
15 | 3
20 | 4
25 | 5

For nickles you count by fives and for quarters you count by ones

Lourdes, on the other hand, seemed to see the relationship between the number of nickels and the number of quarters but did not express it very well. I asked her to explain her thinking to the rest of the class, hoping that others would learn from her explanation. She copied the table from her journal on the board and, with some coaching, explained that 5 times the number of quarters gave the number of nickels. Her journal entry looked like this:

nickels | quarters
5 | 1
10 | 2
15 | 3
20 | 4
25 | 5

They are ~~double~~ 5 times the number. And it goes 1, 2, 3, 4, 5 and 5, 10, 15, 20, 25.

After this discussion, I moved on to another example: "If you have 3 cookies for $1 dollar, how much will 6 cookies cost?" I drew an incomplete table on the board, then once again asked them to complete the table in their journals and write about the patterns and relationships they found.

Cookies | money
3 | $1
6 | $2
9 |

After calling on a couple of students to share what they had written, I asked how many used multiplication to find the pattern. Eleven students raised their hands. "How many used addition?" Twelve students responded. "Drew pictures?" Six students responded. Noticing that Kathleen had not responded, I asked what method she had used. "I counted by 3s," she said.

After praising them for finding so many ways to think about the problem, I gave them another problem to solve independently. As they worked, I walked around observing their work. I was especially proud of Rosa and Askia.

Rosa, who has lived in the United States since September, knows little English and is a student in a "pullout" ESL program. She attended elementary school in Honduras and is a fluent speaker and writer in Spanish. Even though the new vocabulary and our discussion was in English, her work indicated that she might have some understanding of proportional relationships between pairs of ratios.

Rosa's work

Function Mac.

cookis	$
3	$1
6	$2
9	$3
12	$4
15	$5
18	$6
21	$7
24	$8
27	$9
30	$10
33	$11
36	$12
39	$13

$$\frac{3}{1} \qquad \frac{6}{2}$$

$$\frac{9}{3} \qquad \frac{12}{4}$$

$$\frac{15}{5} \qquad \frac{18}{6}$$

$$\frac{21}{7} \qquad \frac{24}{8}$$

$$\frac{27}{30} \qquad \frac{30}{10}$$

yo pienso que
ay una cominasion $\frac{33}{11} \quad \frac{36}{12} \quad \frac{21}{7}$
$3 \rightarrow 39$ otra cominasion
$1 \rightarrow 13$

Because of my limited Spanish, I need the help of my Spanish-speaking students when we discuss her work.

Askia is a resource student who, with lots of encouragement and practice, is beginning to break down his writing inhibitions. I was pleased to see in his writing that he related fractions and ratios; however, I was not sure he or the others understood why we were calling these numbers ratios instead of fractions. I made a mental note to bring this up in the next day's lesson. But after thinking more, I wasn't sure how I could—or if I should—address this issue with fourth graders at all.

Askia's work

I want my classroom and especially my math lessons to encourage risk taking by all students, especially those who for various reasons lack confidence. As I learn how to plan lessons in which diverse methods and solutions are possible, I find that all my students, regardless of their abilities, can participate and discover. Slowly, they are getting the message that open discussion of each others' ideas, even faulty ones, leads us all to better understanding. I am also learning to promote motivation and involvement through the use of hands-on materials, visuals, discussion, and writing. It is satisfying to see these efforts paying off.

Suggested Reading

Azzolino, A. 1990. "Writing as a Tool for Teaching Mathematics: The Silent Revolution." In *Teaching and Learning Mathematics in the 1990s,* edited by T. J. Cooney and C. R. Hirsch, 92–100. Reston, VA: The National Council of Teachers of Mathematics.

Cuevas, G. 1990. "Increasing the Achievement and Participation of Language Minority Students in Mathematics Education." In *Teaching and Learning Mathematics in the 1990s,* edited by T. J. Cooney and C. R. Hirsch, 159–165. Reston, VA: The National Council of Teachers of Mathematics.

Wilde, S. 1991. "Learning to Write About Mathematics." *Arithmetic Teacher* 38(6): 38–43.

Why Isn't It One Less?

A few days ago, my fourth-grade students tackled the following problem as their daily problem-solving activity.

A secondhand store will trade 4 of their comic books for 5 of yours. How many of their comic books will they trade for 35 of yours?

I consciously foster the notion that there are many ways to solve problems by having my students share and discuss their methods. The variety of solutions never ceases to intrigue me. This problem was no exception.

Most students solved this ratio problem by making a table and matching multiples of 4s and 5s until they reached 35. Here are examples of three students' work.

I was somewhat surprised that some of my fourth graders used a more abstract method, which is similar to the method typically used to solve ratio problems. Lee, for example, reasoned that $7 \times 5 = 35$; therefore, 7×4 or 28 would give the answer.

$$\begin{array}{c} 7 \\ \times 5 \\ \hline 35 \end{array} \qquad \begin{array}{c} 7 \\ +4 \\ \hline 28 \end{array} \qquad a = 28$$

Amy had a unique solution. When I asked her to explain her thinking, she said, "I know 7 times 5 is 35, so 35 is 7 groups of your books. Since you get one less of their books for each group of yours, that would be 35 minus 7 or 28."

$$\begin{array}{c} 7 \\ \times 5 \\ \hline 35 \\ - 7 \\ \hline 28 \end{array} \qquad 28 \text{ comic books}$$

At first I wasn't sure if her method made sense or not, so we spent quite a lot of time talking about it.

Karla, another member of the same group, was intrigued by the idea that you could use any operation, addition, subtraction, multiplication, or division, to find the solution "If you knew what you were doing." I was happy to hear this revelation, since at first a lot of my students had thought that to solve a problem you look for key words or plug in an operation based on the size of the numbers in the problem.

While many students demonstrated an understanding of ratios, I was surprised that several students (not the worst math students) said the answer was 34 comic books. I was pretty sure what I was going to hear, but nonetheless I asked for an explanation. Geraldo explained, "It's one less."

I was impressed by the thinking of the children who successfully solved the problem. I felt sure that when confronted by a standard method for solving ratio problems a few years from now, they could much more readily grasp it than if they had not had these kinds of experiences. I wondered if the "one less" people really understood why 34 was incorrect. A few weeks later, my doubts were corroborated. When I assigned a similar problem, many of the "one less" people again subtracted 1 to get their answers. At first, I dismissed their failure by assuming that they were just not ready to comprehend this type of problem. Later, however, I began to wonder whether I could have done more to expand their understanding.

Suggested Reading

Cramer, K., and T. Post. 1993. "Making Connections: A Case for Proportionality." *Arithmetic Teacher* 40(6): 342–346.

Manipulatives Aren't Magic

*When one has no stake in the way things are,
when one's needs or opinions are provided no
forum, when one sees oneself as the object of
unilateral actions, it takes no particular wisdom
to suggest that one would rather be elsewhere.*

SEYMOUR SARASON

Rote Manipulatives?

Some time ago I attended a math conference workshop, the premise of which was that division, percents, proportions, equivalent fractions, and circle-graph computations were all variations of a very important concept: proportionality. In other words, they should be taught as proportions. The presenter asked us to consider a problem where 12 objects were to be divided into 3 fair shares. Adults, she said, used the following form to record the problem and its solution.

$$3 \overline{)\, 12}^{\,4}$$

But using the proportion approach, a problem solver would take the extra step of adding the number 1 to the notation.

$$\overset{①}{3} \overline{)\, 12}^{\,4}$$

Although at first glance this might seem to be a trivial addition, the presenter said, it was crucial. From this new notation two sentences could be formed: "One fair share has 4 objects," and "Three fair shares have 12 objects." The array of numbers could be rewritten as follows:

$$\frac{1}{3} = \frac{4}{12} \text{ or } \frac{1}{4} = \frac{3}{12}$$

In either case we had equivalent fractions, and the cross products in each were 12. Writing the number 1 in the problem gave meaning to the quotient and completes a proportion. As a third year teacher, I was thrilled. I had never looked at division that way, and I found it interesting. Although the lesson that follows was recommended for third graders, I went back to my sixth-grade class determined to reteach division as proportion.

Most of the students in the class were average to low achievers who hadn't had much success with math. I hoped that presenting division as a proportion with concrete models would help them understand the meaning and function of the dividend, divisor, and quotient in *any* problem but particularly when solving word problems.

I told the class we were going to learn how division and proportion were related. They were motivated because proportionality was a new concept. Since this model only works when the division problem doesn't have a remainder, I carefully selected examples and practice problems that had no remainder. This may have been a mistake.

I began by giving them a ministory. Their task was to work with a partner to "build the story" as I told it, using sets of counting cubes. The story began like this: "There are 24 soccer players going to a soccer game." The students counted out 24 cubes to represent soccer players.

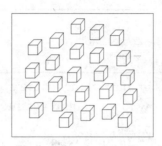

"Now, 2 minivans take the soccer players to the game. Show that, and tell your partner how many soccer players are in each minivan." They placed the cubes in plastic cups representing the minivans.

After I looked at the results, the students told their partners what they had demonstrated: 2 minivans had 24 soccer players, and 1 minivan had 12 soccer players.

We did many similar examples like this together, then moved to the "adult record," which for the same problem would read:

$$\begin{array}{r} 1 \quad 12 \\ \hline 2 \overline{\smash{\big)}\, 24} \end{array}$$

As I began to explain the role of the number 1, I wondered, "Did I teach them to use these manipulatives by rote? And now am I about to show them an algorithm so they can use *it* by rote?"

As we continued with the lesson, one of the higher-achieving students commented, "This is just easy division."

Although it caused me some concern, I ignored her comment and moved on, having students work in pairs to solve problems like this one.

The 8 soccer players in the parking lot are going to the game in two minivans. How many should get into each van?

1 ☐   _____ minivans have _____ soccer players

         _____ minivan has _____ soccer players

Everyone came up with the correct answer.

The 8 soccer players in the parking lot are going to the game in two minivans. How many should get into each van?

1 *4*   *2* minivans have *8* soccer players

2 |*8*| *1* minivan has *4* soccer players

Students' resistance to such "easy" math began to mount as I continued with these lessons. After much reflection, I decided to continue teaching division as a proportion only with a few students who were still having trouble with division. They continued doing this type of work for several more days.

My previous misgivings reappeared when several weeks later Samantha, one of the students who had the extra practice, solved the following problem in class in an interesting but incorrect way. The problem was: "If you have 11 cookies, how can you divide them evenly between 2 people? Solve, explain your answer, and use pictures."

When I asked Samantha to show her answer on the chalkboard, she copied directly from her paper and wrote the following:

If two people have this many cookies . . . (Samantha drew two plates with 11 cookies on each.)

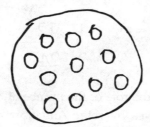

. . . then one person has this
many for their own. (She drew
one plate with 11 cookies.)

When I asked Samantha to explain what she meant, hoping that she would see
her error in the process, she said, "It's just like the soccer players, except I drew
pictures to make it easier. That's okay, isn't it?" To justify her answer, Samantha
wrote the division problem as a proportion on the board.

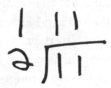

Had the work on proportionality so confused Samantha that she lost the sense
that 11 shared by 2 wouldn't give each person 11?

Suggested Reading

Baroody, A. J. 1989. "Manipulatives Don't Come with Guarantees." *Arithmetic Teacher* 37(2). 4–5.

Driscoll, M., and B. Lord. 1990. "Professionals in a Changing Profession." In *Teaching and Learning Mathematics in the 1990s*, edited by T. J. Cooney and C. R. Hirsch, 237–245. Reston, VA: The National Council of Teachers of Mathematics.

Hiebert, J. 1990. "The Role of Routine Procedures in the Development of Mathematical Competence." In *Teaching and Learning Mathematics in the 1990s*, edited by T. J. Cooney and C. R. Hirsch, 31–40. Reston, VA: The National Council of Teachers of Mathematics.

Two Green Triangles

As I was preparing my lessons after school one day, I remembered a pattern-block activity for teaching fraction concepts. The activity appealed to me because it used a manipulative that interested children, encouraged thinking, and set the stage for further instruction on equivalent fractions. It seemed like an appropriate choice for my fifth graders.

We had already spent several class periods identifying and writing fractions for parts of regions and sets, and all of the students were fairly successful. But I suspected that if I gave them the pattern-block task to complete independently or with a partner, it might overwhelm them. On the other hand, I thought if I approached it in a teacher-directed fashion and we moved slowly enough, they would be successful. It turned out I was wrong.

Since the students had been given ample opportunity to explore pattern blocks at the beginning of the school year, I began by describing the following task: "The yellow hexagon equals 1. Use the other color blocks to make exactly the same size and shape as yellow. Do this as many ways as you can." When some students began making hexagons from more than one color of block, I said I wanted them to use just one color. Several students discovered that the orange and white blocks would not fit into a hexagon, so I suggested they leave those blocks out.

These are the solutions they found:

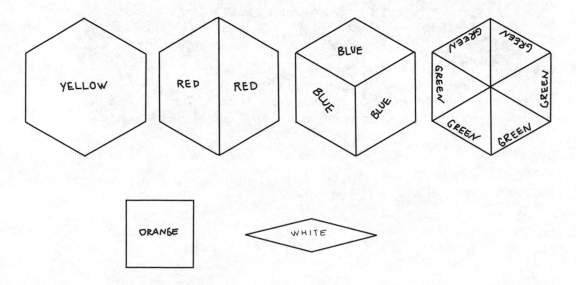

I then displayed the following chart, using the overhead projector. I wrote 1s on the diagonal to show which block was the whole unit for that column. I wanted them to figure out the fractional relationships of the different colored blocks depending on which is considered the whole. My intention was to complete only one or two columns during that class period.

YELLOW	1			
RED		1		
BLUE			1	
GREEN				1

I asked the students which pattern block used the fewest blocks to cover a yellow. They responded, "Red." I asked them how many reds it took to make yellow and they answered, "Two." I told them we needed to write a fractional name for red. I reminded them that yellow was equal to 1 and that it took 2 reds to make yellow, so we would use 2 as our denominator. I wrote "$\frac{}{2}$" on the chart in the first column next to "red." Then I focused their attention on 1 red block and said, "If we have just 1 red block, then 1 is the numerator." I then completed the fraction "$\frac{1}{2}$" on the chart as illustrated below.

YELLOW	1			
RED	$\frac{1}{2}$	1		
BLUE			1	
GREEN				1

I pointed to the $\frac{1}{2}$ on the chart and asked how we say that fraction. They responded, "One-half." They appeared to be very comfortable with the concept of red as $\frac{1}{2}$ of yellow.

Then I held up a blue and asked students how many blues make a yellow. They responded 3, and I wrote "$\frac{}{3}$" in the chart next to "blue." Then, still holding up the blue block, I asked, "How many thirds is this?"

"One," they all agreed, and I wrote a 1 in the numerator to show "$\frac{1}{3}$". We continued the same painstaking process for the green block.

YELLOW	1		
RED	$\frac{1}{2}$	1	
BLUE	$\frac{1}{3}$		1
GREEN	$\frac{1}{6}$		1

I felt confident that the students understood that the red was $\frac{1}{2}$ of the yellow, blue was $\frac{1}{3}$ of the yellow, and green was $\frac{1}{6}$ of the yellow. I decided to check their understanding a little further. I held up 2 green triangles and said, "If yellow equals 1 then how much is this?"

The boys and girls responded in unison, "Two."

"Two what?" I asked, hoping to hear "sixths."

They looked a bit confused and then one child said, "TWO GREEN TRIANGLES!" They all happily agreed.

I held up the 2 green triangles and said, "If these are less than yellow, it wouldn't make sense to call them 2. We need to write a fraction using a numerator and a denominator. How do we do that?" I could see by the expressions on their faces that they were really stumped. We went back to how many greens equal yellow and the fractional name for 1 green triangle. It seemed like the only way they could name or write the fractions was if I asked the questions and they filled in the blanks. Why?

Suggested Reading

Ball, D. L. 1991. "'What's All This Talk About Discourse?': Implementing the Professional Standards for Teaching Mathematics." *Arithmetic Teacher* 39(8): 14–48.

Donovan, B. F. 1990. "Cultural Power and the Defining of School Mathematics: A Case Study." In *Teaching and Learning Mathematics in the 1990s*, edited by T. J. Cooney and C. R. Hirsch, 166–173. Reston, VA: The National Council of Teachers of Mathematics.

Yackel, E., P. Cobb, T. Wood, G. Wheatley, and G. Merkel. 1990. "The Importance of Social Interaction in Children's Construction of Mathematical Knowledge." In *Teaching and Learning Mathematics in the 1990s*, edited by T. J. Cooney and C. R. Hirsch, 12–21. Reston, VA: The National Council of Teachers of Mathematics.

What Next?

*A teacher affects eternity; he can never
tell where his influence stops.*

HENRY BROOKS ADAMS

Where Do I Go from Here?

The year I transferred from elementary to junior-high teaching, I read several *Arithmetic Teacher* articles on the importance of writing in mathematics. I also attended two workshops on improving students' understanding of fractions through visualization and verbalization. I was intrigued to find out how these principles might be applied in my new classroom with students who were accustomed to traditional textbook-oriented teaching and generally lacked self-confidence in mathematics. I knew the idea of talking and writing about their mathematical thoughts would seem quite foreign.

In the fall we had begun a three-week unit on decimal concepts. My pretest indicated that the students were fairly competent with problems that asked them to compare two decimals. After a few days of whole-class discussions about decimal place value and several lessons on using graph paper to draw decimal amounts, I made my first writing assignment.

> *Why is 0.292 less than 0.3?*
> 1. *Explain in a paragraph.*
> 2. *Draw a picture.*

The results were informative but a little disappointing. About a third of the students lacked comprehension of the basic concepts related to depicting decimal amounts and the comparison of quantities. Their misconceptions were so diverse and complex that I found it difficult to know how to address them.

Joe, for example, compared a huge square to show 0.292 (which was actually 0.2902) and a tiny square to show 0.3 (which he drew as 30 squares out of a 100).

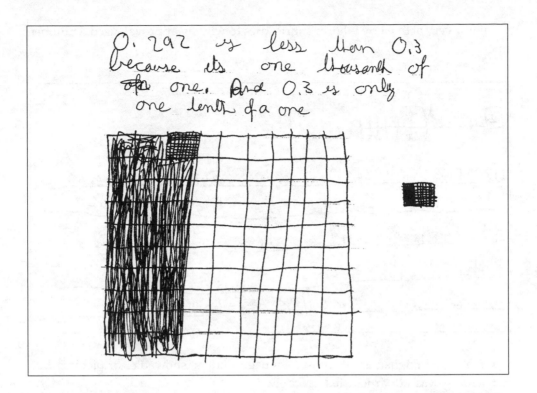

0. 292 is less than 0.3
because its one thousandth of
of a one. And 0.3 is only
one tenth of a one

I had difficulty interpreting a number of the papers. Some students minimized the drawing and essentially stated a rule for comparing decimals. Melanie, who experiences frequent frustration in class as she searches for a rule to associate with every task, wrote:

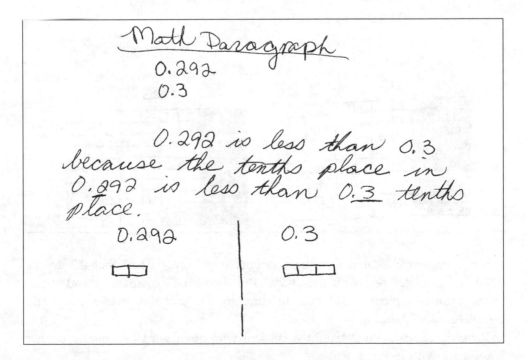

Math Paragraph

0.292
0.3

0.292 is less than 0.3 because the tenths place in 0.292 is less than 0.3 tenths place.

0.292 | 0.3

Jake, a very active boy who, in spurts, tries to win my approval, used a number line.

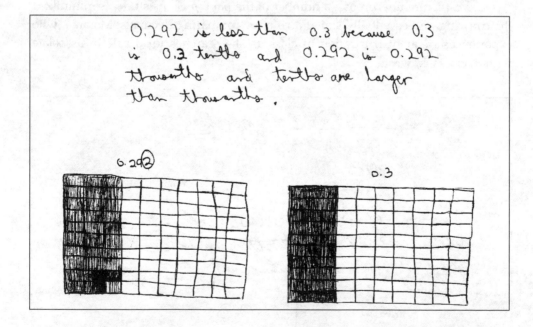

② [number line]

① The veson .3 is biger then .292 is that 3 tenths is biger then 292 thoseths and tenths are biger hundreths or thosenths and .2 is smaller than .3?

Carolyn, an English-as-a-Second-Language student, showed clear pictures, but her writing was not articulated precisely.

0.292 is less than 0.3 because 0.3 is 0.3 tenths and 0.292 is 0.292 thousanths and tenths are larger than thousanths.

0.292   0.3

Some papers indicated that their authors *might* understand that 0.3 equals 0.300 and is therefore greater than 0.292. But their brief explanations and sometimes erroneous pictures did little to convince me that they had a deep and complete understanding.

Rebecca, an energetic, straight-A student who often works diligently on her homework with her dad, wrote:

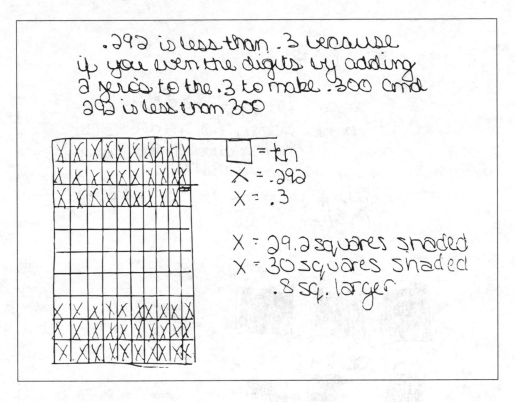

.292 is less than .3 because
if you even the digits by adding
2 zeros to the .3 to make .300 and
292 is less than 300

☐ = ten
X = .292
X = .3

X = 29.2 squares shaded
X = 30 squares shaded
.8 sq. larger

Carl, who refuses to take school seriously, submitted:

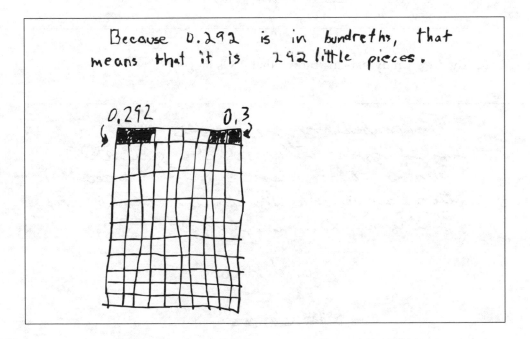

Because 0.292 is in hundreths, that
means that it is 292 little pieces.

0.292   0.3

When I asked Susan, a resource student, to explain her drawing, she said she
drew the "flat" from the base-10 blocks to show each tenth.

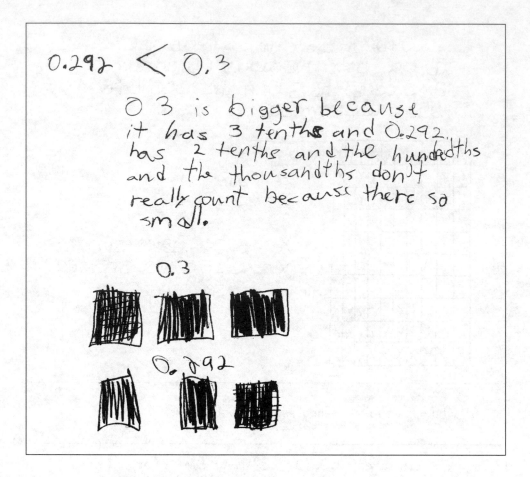

$0.292 < 0.3$

0.3 is bigger because it has 3 tenths and 0.292 has 2 tenths and the hundreths and the thousandths don't really count because there so small.

0.3

0.292

Randy drew candy bars to "prove" that 0.3 is bigger.

1. The number on the right 0.3 is bigger than 0.292 cause 0.3 means three lenths. 0.292 means two and 92 thousands. Thats why I think 0.3 is bigger.

2. candy bars

0.3 — [candy] [candy] [candy]
0.292— [candy] [candy] [can]

that proves 0.3 is bigger

George, who never conforms to class norms, submitted:

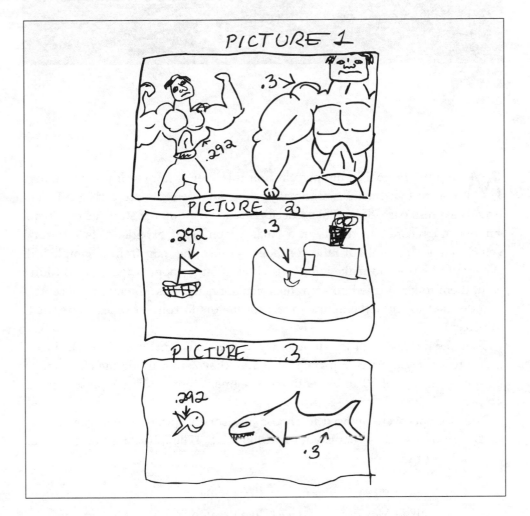

I found myself wondering "Where do I go from here?"

Suggested Reading

Clarke, D. J., D. M. Clarke, and C. J. Lovitt. 1990. "Changes in Mathematics Teaching Call for Assessment Alternatives." In *Teaching and Learning Mathematics in the 1990s*, edited by T. J. Cooney and C. R. Hirsch, 118–129. Reston, VA: The National Council of Teachers of Mathematics.

Sullivan, P., and D. Clarke. 1991. "Catering to All Abilities Through 'Good' Questions." *Arithmetic Teacher* 39(2): 14–18.

Favorite-Food Circle Graph

My primary goal in my percent unit this year is to help my sixth graders realize that fractions, decimals, ratios, and percents are each a different way to express parts of a whole. I decided to have groups of students conduct a survey and record the results in a circle graph. That experience is a natural vehicle for learning about ratio concepts, because the data from a sample will eventually be used to make inferences about a larger population. Since I didn't want them to get bogged down in the calculation and miss the major concepts, I also decided to show them how to use calculators to convert ratios to decimals to percents.

To make the results of the survey easy to draw on a circle graph, I asked each group to survey exactly 36 people. That way they could divide the circle graph into 36 segments of 10° each, with each segment representing 1 person in the survey.

The students were allowed to choose any survey question they wanted. Estrella's group asked, "What is your favorite food?" The following ratios showed the results of their poll.

$\frac{22}{36}$ liked pizza $\frac{2}{36}$ liked tamales

$\frac{3}{36}$ liked Mexican food $\frac{2}{36}$ liked seafood

$\frac{3}{36}$ liked chicken $\frac{1}{36}$ liked lasagna

$\frac{2}{36}$ liked hamburgers $\frac{1}{36}$ liked tostadas

During the next class period we talked about the meaning of 100%, and everyone seemed comfortable with the idea that 100% meant all of the people in the survey. I discussed with them that since 100% is a whole, 1% would be the same as one hundredth. I told them that decimals rounded to the nearest hundredth would be the same as a percentage. For example, 0.38 would be the same as 38%.

We then used calculators to convert some sample ratios to decimals, dividing the numerator by the denominator. Then, I reminded them how to round each decimal to the nearest hundredth to find the percent. Several students had difficulty rounding the decimals to the nearest hundredth and needed to review this skill. I made up several examples, and most students were able to change the ratio to a decimal and convert the rounded decimal to a percent—until they got to $\frac{5}{25}$. When they divided 5 by 25 on the calculator, they got 0.2, which they said was 2%. This was a snag I hadn't expected, but we worked through it, reviewing that two tenths is equivalent to twenty hundredths. Thus, 0.2 would be the same as 20%.

The following day, everyone seemed confident and eager to start work on their survey data. They began by converting their ratios to percentages with calculators. Once this was done, they made circle graphs and recorded their results in ratios and percents. Estrella's group made the following circle graph which they entitled "Favorite Food."

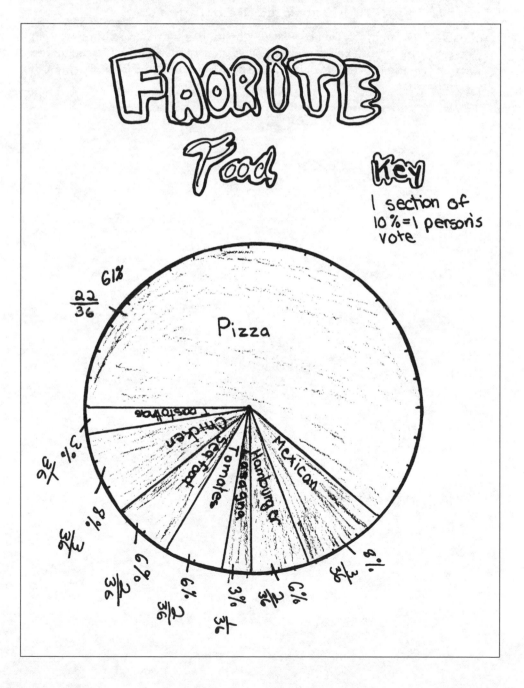

As I looked through the graphs, I realized that there was some confusion. For example, the key for the graph made by Estrella's group showed that they didn't really understand what each of the 36 sections on the graph represented. Nonetheless, I felt that the main thrust of the next day's discussion should be about ratio and percent equivalents. I also wondered about the role of the calculator—whether it helped students focus on the concept. How could I find out?

Suggested Reading

Allinger, G. D., and J. N. Payne. 1986. "Estimation and Mental Arithmetic with Percent." In *Estimation and Mental Computation*, edited by H. L. Schoen and M. J. Zweng, 141–155. Reston, VA: The National Council of Teachers of Mathematics.

What's My Grade?

I make sure that throughout the year my fifth graders have informal opportunities to learn about percent. For example, during the first week of school they learn how to use a calculator to determine the percent of correct answers on their assignments, dividing the number of correct answers by the total number of questions. They also learn how, at the end of each week, to compute the average percent of correct answers on all of the week's assignments.

We also explore how zero percent—for a missing or incomplete assignment—affects their grades. We calculate the average percent of a given set of grades and then recalculate after a zero percent is added to the total. It is always a revelation to the students to watch how rapidly a grade drops as more zeros are added. These informal experiences lay the foundation for a percent unit presented during the spring.

One Friday, shortly before the end of the second grading period, Phillip came up to me with a paper clutched in his hand. I could tell by his expression that he was upset.

"How come I got a 'C' on this paper when I only got two problems wrong?" he asked.

Phillip is very concerned about his grades. He comes from a middle-class, professional black family and is under a lot of pressure to perform to their rigid standards. I really didn't know how to respond, but I briefly explained how the number of problems in an assignment relates to the percent—this assignment had only eight problems. Kids usually say my grading is reasonable and fair, so I think he may have just accepted my explanation on faith. I made a mental note to myself to be sure to address this important concept further when we did our percent unit in the spring.

We've just finished an introductory unit on ratios and proportions begun early this spring. Now, I'm preparing to teach the unit on percent. I want to change my approach this year to do a better job building the fundamental idea of percent and addressing misconceptions such as the one underlying Phillip's confusion earlier in the year. In the past, I've introduced the idea of percent through graph-paper models of 100 squares. The students color in some of the squares and then name the percent of the squares that are colored. They see that 35 squares out of 100 is 35%, 17 squares is 17%, and so on. Then I show them how to write a percent as a fraction or a decimal. For example, 75% is the same as 0.75, $\frac{75}{100}$ (or $\frac{3}{4}$ in lowest terms). Once this is understood, we go on to finding a percent of a number. Since they know that "of" means "multiply" in fraction multiplication, I taught them to do the same thing with percent. To find 20% of 40, they are taught to change 20% to a decimal or a fraction and then multiply. This series of lessons takes four or five days. Although my students have had ongoing informal experiences with percent and are very successful on these lessons, the "Phillips" in my class still don't realize that the percent score for missing 2 out of 8 is much lower than for missing 2 out of 40. I would like to find a more effective teaching strategy that addresses this issue.

Suggested Reading

Allinger, G. D., and J. N. Payne. 1986. "Estimation and Mental Arithmetic with Percent." In *Estimation and Mental Computation*, edited by H. L. Schoen and M. J. Zweng, 141–155. Reston, VA: The National Council of Teachers of Mathematics.

Connections

The horizon leans forward,
Offering you space
To place new steps of change
Here, on the pulse of this fine day

MAYA ANGELOU

Percents, Proportions, and Grids

I have had a great deal of difficulty teaching the three types of percent problems:

What is 15% of 20?
What % of 20 is 3?
3 is 15% of what number?

Early in my teaching career, I used to teach my students to solve these problems the same way I had learned them. In the first type, students were taught to rename the percent as a decimal by moving the decimal point two places to the left and multiplying the two numbers together. In the second and third types, students were taught to divide the two numbers. This method was unsuccessful since many students could not remember when to multiply or when to divide, or, when they had to divide, which number was to be divided by which. I also taught students to solve these problems using equations. Regardless of which way I taught it, I had a nagging feeling that if the students came up with the correct answers it was only because they were able to manipulate the numbers. I was convinced there must a better way to teach percents.

This year I decided to teach percents through proportions. My students are ninth graders who are at least two years below grade level in math and have not passed a sixth-grade-level computation proficiency test. After a two-week review unit on ratio, proportion, and percent equivalencies, we began a lesson on the first type of percent problem: What is 15% of 20?

To show them how to find 15% of 20, I asked the students to draw a 10-by-10 grid on a piece of graph paper and then show 15% by shading in the appropriate number of "little parts." Then, I asked the students to draw a second square the same size as the first but divided into 20 equal parts. I then asked, "How many of those 20 parts would represent the same amount as the shaded part in the first square?" Most students shaded in two parts of the first strip and one part of the second strip. I then asked them to count the total number of shaded parts out of the 20 in the whole square. Since 3 parts in the second grid represent the same amount shaded in the first grid, I concluded that 3 parts represent 15% of 20.

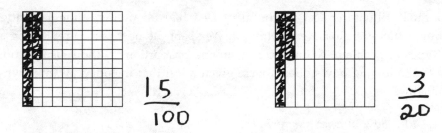

I then asked the students to write an equality to represent the relationship between the two squares: $\frac{15}{100} = \frac{3}{20}$

We spent a couple of days doing this type of problem, and then I taught students how to write and solve the related proportion by using cross multiplication: $\frac{15}{100} = \frac{x}{20}$, where x represents 15% of 20.

We then began work on the second type of percent problem: What percent of 20 is 3? Once again, I had my students use grids to help them write and solve proportions.

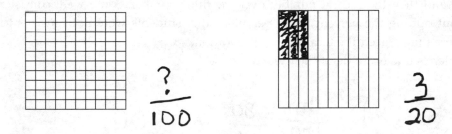

They seemed to understand that we wrote $\frac{x}{100} = \frac{3}{20}$ or "x over 100" because we didn't know how many parts are in the left-hand grid. They also knew how to shade the same area on both grids to see that x was equal to 15 little squares or 15%.

The students spent the following class period doing this type of problem without the use of grids, and they seemed to have no trouble setting up and solving the proportions. I felt confident we could move on to the last type of percent problem: 3 is 15% of what number?

Nearly every student began shading in 15 squares in the first 10-by-10 grid. I asked a couple of students why they shaded the 15 squares. Both responded identically, "Because 15% means 15 out of 100!" I noticed that some were then shading in 3 squares of the second grid. Another group was trying to divide the 10-by-10 grid into 3 equal parts. Many students decided that this problem was not like the other ones, but they didn't know how to proceed.

Clearly, this third type of percent problem posed more difficulty for the class than I had anticipated. So, I decided to do the problem together, and during the rest of the period we worked through similar problems using the grids. In the following period, we worked on setting up proportions for this type of problem.

Although I still didn't feel as confident as I had about the students' understanding, I thought most were getting it. We spent the next period reviewing all three types of problem, setting up and solving proportions without using grids.

On the following day students were given a test that included all three types of problems.

1. 40 is 80% of what number?
2. 35% of 80 is what number?
3. 18 is what % of 45?
4. 40 is what % of 60?
5. 20% of what number is 16?
6. What is 85% of 12?

The results were disappointing, but I don't know how I could have better prepared them. In analyzing their work, I noticed that only about half the students were able to set up the proportions correctly. Some students set up the proportion by always putting the first number that appeared in the problem over 100 and then the second number over the third number. Some were consistent about putting the percent term over 100. Other students were not consistent in where they placed the terms in the proportion.

Here's one example of their test responses:

$$\checkmark 1) \quad \frac{40}{100} = \frac{80}{x} \quad x = 200$$

$$\checkmark 2) \quad \frac{35}{100} = \frac{80}{x} \quad x = 22$$

$$\checkmark 3) \quad \frac{45}{1} = \frac{x}{100} \quad x = 40\%$$

$$4. \quad \frac{40}{100} = \frac{60}{x} \quad x = \boxed{150} \checkmark$$

$$5. \quad \frac{16}{100} = \frac{x}{20} \quad x = \boxed{32} \checkmark$$

$$6. \quad \frac{85}{100} = \frac{12}{x} \quad x = \boxed{14.117647} \checkmark$$

Based on the test results, I can't help feeling that once again I have a group of students who are merely manipulating numbers without understanding. I even wonder if those students who did the problems correctly actually understood them or whether they set up the proportions correctly simply by memorizing a pattern.

The next time I teach percent problems, I think I need to invest more time developing an understanding of proportions. I'm not sure whether the grids were effective or if I should use a different model. As part of their ongoing assignments, I would also like to ask the students for written explanations of how they did the problems. Perhaps requiring them to reflect on and break down their thinking processes would increase their understanding. I am worried, though, because we have a limited amount of time, and these students are already at least two years behind. I wonder whether it will ever be possible to make my students proficient with all three types of percent problems.

Suggested Reading

Allinger, G. D., and J. N. Payne. 1986. "Estimation and Mental Arithmetic with Percent." In *Estimation and Mental Computation*, edited by H. L. Schoen and M. J. Zweng, 141–155. Reston, VA: The National Council of Teachers of Mathematics.

Janvier, C. 1990. "Contextualization and Mathematics for All." In *Teaching and Learning Mathematics in the 1990s*, edited by T. J. Cooney and C. R. Hirsch, 183–193. Reston, VA: The National Council of Teachers of Mathematics.

Six Hours Isn't One-Sixth of a Day

In February, I began my first year of teaching. My class was a straight fourth grade. As a recent graduate, I was gung ho on using manipulatives and cooperative teaching methods. I was hired midyear due to overcrowded classrooms, and I inherited twenty-eight students from two different classrooms. These students were reasonably competent with multiplication, simple division, and basic fractions. They knew the algorithms but had almost no previous experience with math manipulatives or cooperative math groups. To review their basic fractions and fraction equivalency, I had them make fraction kits with halves, fourths, thirds, sixths, and eighths. After working with the kits for several class sessions, I felt my students were ready to extend their work with fraction equivalency by applying it to circle graphs.

Working in cooperative math groups formed from one high, one low, and two mid-level students, they were asked to reach a consensus on how much time, to the nearest whole hour, they spend in a 24-hour period on the following activities: sleeping, eating, going to school, playing, and watching TV. Each group successfully colored and labeled a large circle graph which had been predivided into 24 sections.

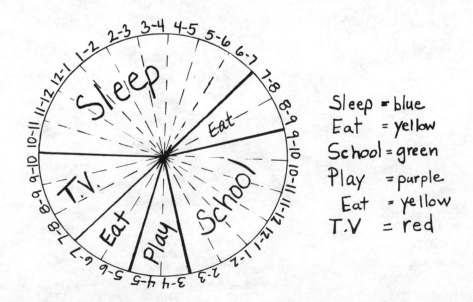

Sleep = blue
Eat = yellow
School = green
Play = purple
Eat = yellow
T.V = red

The next day, I put their colored graphs on the board along with an extra predivided circle for reference.

"Looking at the graphs divided into 24 hour sections, can you see any way we could use fractions to talk about these graphs?" I was hoping that they would recognize that the sections were 24ths, or realize that 12 hours represented $\frac{1}{2}$ of a day and 6 hours represented $\frac{1}{4}$ of a day.

Jason quickly shouted out, "Yeah, 12 hours is half a day!" Nods of agreement came from most of the class. I then wrote the following on the board: 12 hours $= \frac{1}{2}$ of a day. Allowing for the appropriate amount of thinking time, I waited for another revelation. Nothing!

"Is there a fraction we could write to represent the entire graph?" All was quiet as several students began counting sections.

"Twenty-fours," Jason quickly responded.

I wrote on the board: 1 day = _____. "How shall I write the fraction?"

Susan said, "One twenty-fourth."

"No," corrected Lisa, "it's twenty-four twenty-fours." I wrote $\frac{24}{24}$ on the board.

"Does everyone agree with that fractional representation of a day?" The class indicated acceptance. I was relieved that they seemed to realize that a name for the whole day was a key place to start. I expected the students to generate other fractions at least with a denominator of 24. I asked if there were other fractions we could use to represent the various sections of the graph. They studied the graph, but there were no more spontaneous responses.

"Let's look at the sections colored green on this graph for the time spent in school. How many———?"

Jason interrupted, "Six hours."

"Can you give me a fraction to represent those 6 hours?" Again students counted sections aloud.

"Six hours equals one-sixth," responded Karen. A nod of agreement came from around the class. Not one student came up with $\frac{6}{24}$, let alone $\frac{1}{4}$.

I was counting on the visual cues from the models to trigger some recognition of the fractions represented. Except for Jason noticing that 12 hours was $\frac{1}{2}$ of a day, they obviously didn't "see" these relationships. I also expected them to remember how to name fractions based on our work with the fraction kits over the past couple weeks. There seemed to be almost no transfer. I'd like to know why.

Suggested Reading

Behr, M. J., T. R. Post, and I. Wachsmuth. 1986. "Estimation and Children's Concept of Rational Number Size." In *Estimation and Mental Computation*, edited by H. L. Schoen and M. J. Zweng, 103–111. Reston, VA: The National Council of Teachers of Mathematics.

Woodcock, G. E. 1986. "Estimating Fractions: A Picture is Worth a Thousand Words." In *Estimation and Mental Computation*, edited by H. L. Schoen and M. J. Zweng, 112–115. Reston, VA: The National Council of Teachers of Mathematics.

This Wasn't My Plan

The front of a classroom is a powerful place to be.
The responsibility is awesome. You cannot teach and
empower children to be successful if you do not hold
yourself to be so. Everything you are and all that you
believe is transmitted to your students at some level.

PATRICIA MUNSON

Bubbles to Kickball

Part One

As a beginner working in another teacher's room, I had very little knowledge of these sixth-grade students' math backgrounds. I wanted to do a math lesson that was fun, hands on, not dependent on their past experiences, and not just paper and pencil work. When I found a lesson using bubbles in a science unit, I decided to make it a "math lesson" by emphasizing the concept and term *diameter* in my presentation. Bill, the classroom teacher, said they probably had many experiences with diameter but might not have heard or used the term itself before. I remembered later that he also once said "they've had decimals" without elaborating further.

I explained that their task was to blow bubbles with each of three different liquid soap brands to find out which brand made the biggest bubbles. I demonstrated how to blow a bubble by pouring some soap solution on a cutting board and blowing into the solution with a straw. This formed a bubble on the cutting board.

When the bubble popped, it left a circle of residue on the cutting board. We then talked about how to measure the diameter of that ring. I probed for their understanding of the concept of diameter by suggesting a series of incorrect and correct representations: I held up the cutting board and laid a ruler across the ring at various angles, while they called out yes and no in response to my question, "Is this a diameter?" Judging by their responses, they knew exactly what was and was not a correct representation of diameter. We also talked informally about why or why not a particular representation was correct. I prompted them towards postulating that it had to pass through a middle point and that the lengths on either side of that point had to be equal.

I instructed them to blow four different bubbles with each of the three solutions and gave them a sheet to write down the measures of each diameter. The sheet also had a place for them to record the average of the 4 diameters for each solution. Although the ultimate goal was to compare the size of bubbles blown from the three different brands, I didn't realize until later that this lesson also involved average. I had not anticipated nor planned for this in my presentation.

Even though I was a little worried about how the students would handle so much freedom and the potential for a very wet disaster, I assigned groups and roles such as station monitor and supplies monitor and then let them go. Since I was new at teaching, I didn't know how much they respected my directions or how well they would behave in a situation like this. I was also worried that these urban city kids, some living in the toughest and most poverty-stricken parts of town, would find bubbles patronizing.

Everything was going great. Despite some pockets of spurious bubble blowing—to be expected—the kids were having a fantastic time blowing and measuring the bubbles, and most were filling in their sheets. After fifteen minutes, students began bringing their results to me to check. Despite how pleased I was with their excitement and my initial success, I discovered that every group but one had incorrectly computed the average of their measurements, most making the exact same kind of error.

I called on Paige to show us her work, knowing that the answer she got was a nonwhole number. She went to the board and divided 25 total inches by 4 measurements, wrote 6 above the 5, subtracted 24, found a remainder of 1, put a decimal point after the 6, and wrote in the remainder 1 following the point.

$$4\overline{)25} \begin{array}{c} 6.1 \\ \hline \end{array} = 6.1 \text{ in}$$
$$\underline{24}$$
$$1$$

I asked the class if the answer was correct and stood there waiting for someone to see her mistake. The whole class called out yes, but then shrugged their shoulders in acquiescence when I didn't confirm their convictions. They didn't recognize the mistake; but they knew something was up. I waited a little bit longer.

All of a sudden, I realized that I was about to tell them exactly what they did wrong, but I managed to catch myself. Through my courses at the university and work with a mathematics professional development project, I had learned that it was more valuable to allow students to investigate on their own rather than simply telling them the answer and expecting them to absorb it. I was hoping to see this technique actually work in practice, after only hearing and reading about it outside of the classroom.

I continued by asking if anyone knew how to check division problems. They were slow, but a few were timidly saying, "Multiply." I suggested that we check the answer I had written and asked Jessica to do the multiplication with a calculator. I asked if the class answer, 24.40, showed that our division was correct. Some reluctantly replied no, others reluctantly replied yes. I told them that it wasn't correct and asked, "Now that we know it's wrong, what should we do?" I waited and again no one seemed to have any ideas.

Then I asked if they knew how to find a fraction answer to this problem. I remembered that a few had done it this way correctly on the data sheet. Marco led me through the problem, finding $6\frac{1}{4}$ as the answer. I asked if they knew how to translate the fractional part into a decimal. After a few seconds, one or two students replied, "point 25." I asked if 6.25 was equal to 6.1. A few students replied, "No." I stated that since these are not equal one must be wrong. Then I hesitated and wasn't sure where to go from there. The students weren't seeing their mistake through this method, although they seemed to be convinced their answer was wrong.

Finally, I decided just to present the algorithm. I asked Melisha to walk me through another problem (without a whole answer), offering the correct procedure when she was unsure. When we finished, a few kids shouted they hadn't seen it or didn't understand. By this time I was feeling guilty for "giving up" and showing them the algorithm anyway—I wasn't about to go through it again. So I attempted to generate a little understanding of what we were doing. I asked the class what the remainder in the first problem was. One said it was 1 tenth. Most were silent and either did not understand or were unable to express the difficult concept of remainder.

Finally, Reggie answered "One is 25 hundredths of 4." I knew this was a hot lead and waited for another student to respond, but no one picked up his lead, including me. I couldn't figure out how to expand on what he said. Perhaps I could have rephrased it or asked another student a question about it. I knew it was significant, but I didn't have the resources to capitalize on it. The bell rang, and I was a little relieved that I would have some time to think about what to do next.

Part Two

After class, I began to think that the students clearly needed help in averages, but I had to somehow make averages more relevant to their lives. I needed to find an example that they had more experience with. Later that evening, I devised a plan to work on averages using statistics from the school's weekly kickball game. The following Friday, game day, I brought in a sheet for the class to keep statistics on the players. Students worked in groups but kept individual records to be shared with those six students who played in the game. I hoped this was the real-life example that could make the averages and decimal quotients clear to them.

In class after the game, I asked the students to work in groups to decide how many hits each player from our class had gotten and how many times they had gotten up to kick. Then, I asked them to talk about how they would find each player's average. Soon we got into a whole-group discussion.

I asked the class, "If I got up 4 times and only got 1 hit, what would my average be?" I wrote the statistics on the overhead using *AB* for "at bat," *H* for "hit," and *AVG* for "average" from baseball statistics.

AB	H	AVG
4	1	

A few students answered, "two-fifty," and I wrote .250 on the board under AVG. Many of them insisted it was "two-hundred and fifty." I finally got most to agree it was twenty-five hundredths. Rigo, a very intelligent and sports-oriented student, asked why the announcers always say "two-fifty." I explained that they're just shortening it and that they *mean* twenty-five hundredths. I realized that the way these students have always heard these averages pronounced is not mathematically accurate. I also realized that I had probably incorrectly assumed that the students knew that "two-fifty" was written .250 in sports averages.

We worked through the division problem on the board to help them see how to compute the average. I went on to ask another question that attempted to get at their understanding of the concept of average. What if I got up 3 times and I got 2 hits? I wrote the statistics on the overhead as I did before.

AB	H	AVG
3	2	

At first, one student reported that the average was 1.5. I asked her how you could get $1\frac{1}{2}$ hits every time you got up, which only confused her more. I realized she and probably many other students didn't have a clue as to what a correct answer to this problem looked like. Some students complained they kept getting

6 (in the tenths place, the hundredths place and so on), while others said they couldn't get rid of 2 as a remainder.

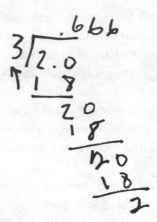

I was frustrated and off track. I just sat there and laughed at myself and the absurdity of the situation. I had generated more confusion and misunderstandings than I could deal with. I had been attempting to follow up on the students' difficulties with the bubble lesson but had gotten into even more trouble. I realized that the kickball averages were an inappropriate follow-up to the first lesson, because they brought out even more confusing issues. I wondered if experienced teachers run into these same kind of problems.

Suggested Reading

Rowan, T. E., and N. D. Cetorelli. 1990. "An Eclectic Model for Teaching Elementary School Mathematics." In *Teaching and Learning Mathematics in the 1990s*, edited by T. J. Cooney and C. R. Hirsch, 62–68. Reston, VA: The National Council of Teachers of Mathematics.

The Beauty of Math

The students in my seventh- and eighth-grade pre-algebra classes had spent considerable time studying fractions and various properties, including inverse operations. They had a fairly firm understanding of these concepts, and I wanted to challenge them with some mathematical explorations that provided opportunities to apply these ideas in different ways. They enjoy this kind of challenge since they are high achievers, quick learners, and most have qualified for Gifted And Talented Education (GATE) status.

Some of my favorite explorations are with a special set of unit fractions (fractions with 1 in the numerator). To identify one of the fractions in the special set, you write a 1 in the numerator and a product of two consecutive numbers in the denominator (For example, $\frac{1}{1\cdot2}$). So, 1 over the product of 1 and 2 makes the unit fraction $\frac{1}{2}$; 1 over the product of 2 and 3 makes the next unit fraction $\frac{1}{6}$, and so on.

$$\frac{1}{1\cdot2} = \frac{1}{2}$$

$$\frac{1}{2\cdot3} = \frac{1}{6}$$

$$\frac{1}{3\cdot4} = \frac{1}{12}$$

$$\frac{1}{4\cdot5} = \frac{1}{20}$$

$$\frac{1}{5\cdot6} = \frac{1}{30}$$

One of the mathematically interesting things about these special fractions is that they can all be expressed as the difference between two unit fractions. The denominators of these unit fractions are the same as those used to generate the fraction. So, 1 over the product of 1 and 2 is equivalent to 1 over 1 minus 1 over 2; 1 over the product of 2 and 3 is equivalent to 1 over 2 minus 1 over 3, and so on.

$$\frac{1}{1\cdot2} = \frac{1}{2} = \left(\frac{1}{1} - \frac{1}{2}\right)$$

$$\frac{1}{2\cdot3} = \frac{1}{6} = \left(\frac{1}{2} - \frac{1}{3}\right)$$

$$\frac{1}{3 \cdot 4} = \frac{1}{12} = \left(\frac{1}{3} - \frac{1}{4}\right)$$

$$\frac{1}{4 \cdot 5} = \frac{1}{20} = \left(\frac{1}{4} - \frac{1}{5}\right)$$

$$\frac{1}{5 \cdot 6} = \frac{1}{30} = \left(\frac{1}{5} - \frac{1}{6}\right)$$

We took several math periods to talk about the mathematics in this exploration, including the commutative and associative properties, the use of different mathematical operations, and definitions of words like *consecutive* and *sequential*. I also had them identify patterns and relationships among the equations and spent some time going over inverse operations, showing them how to "cancel out" a number by adding its opposite.

The students had maintained a high level of interest, and I decided it was time to show them the "connectedness" in math. I pulled out my "beautiful" problem. We've had numerous "beautiful" problems before, and I could hardly wait to give them the directions. The problem I had in mind would pull everything together . . .

I called for their attention and explained that I wanted to assess their mastery of fraction operations by having them solve and write about a problem that had a little of everything we had been talking about for the past few days. I wrote the following problem on the board and asked them to solve it in their cooperative groups.

$$\frac{1}{1 \cdot 2} + \frac{1}{2 \cdot 3} + \frac{1}{3 \cdot 4} + \frac{1}{4 \cdot 5} + \frac{1}{5 \cdot 6}$$

The students were asked to solve the problem, if they could, using any of the methods we had used earlier—properties, inverse operations, cancellations, etc. "Then," I informed them, "I'd like you to explain why the problem works." Finally, I informed them that they could solve the problem in other ways, even the conventional way, if they could not solve it using the method we had explored in class today.

After approximately twenty minutes, I asked the different groups to give me their solutions and answers. Unsurprisingly, most had the correct answer, but surprisingly only one group had solved the problem using an inverse operation, the commutative property, or the associative property.

Most had solved the problem using the following method.

$$\frac{1}{1 \cdot 2} = \frac{1}{2} = \frac{30}{60}$$

$$\frac{1}{2 \cdot 3} = \frac{1}{6} = \frac{10}{60}$$

$$\frac{1}{3 \cdot 4} = \frac{1}{12} = \frac{5}{60}$$

$$\frac{1}{4\cdot5} = \frac{1}{20} = \frac{3}{60}$$

$$\frac{1}{5\cdot6} = \frac{1}{30} = \frac{2}{60}$$

Using a common denominator of 60, they had finally added to get $\frac{50}{60}$ and reduced the answer to $\frac{5}{6}$ by scratching the zeros.

Another group had solved the problem in the following manner:

$$\frac{1}{1\cdot2} + \frac{1}{2\cdot3} + \frac{1}{3\cdot4} + \frac{1}{4\cdot5} + \frac{1}{5\cdot6} =$$

$$\frac{1}{2} + \frac{1}{6} + \frac{1}{12} + \frac{1}{20} + \frac{1}{30} =$$

$$2 + 6 + 12 + 20 + 30 = 70$$

Neither I nor the group was sure of the reasoning behind this answer. After reviewing their answers, I wrote my method of solving the problem on the board.

$$\frac{1}{1\cdot2} + \frac{1}{2\cdot3} + \frac{1}{3\cdot4} + \frac{1}{4\cdot5} + \frac{1}{5\cdot6} =$$

$$\left(\frac{1}{1} - \frac{1}{2}\right) + \left(\frac{1}{2} - \frac{1}{3}\right) + \left(\frac{1}{3} - \frac{1}{4}\right) + \left(\frac{1}{4} - \frac{1}{5}\right) + \left(\frac{1}{5} - \frac{1}{6}\right) =$$

I proceeded to ask the students if they recognized any "opposites" in the equation. They did. As they revealed them to me, I canceled them out.

Eventually, we had the following equation.

$$1 - \frac{1}{6} = \frac{5}{6}$$

Jade commented: "I didn't know we could cancel. You should have said we could use what you did at the beginning of the period."

What I had meant to be a lesson on the beauty of math had gotten lost. Most students had turned this rich problem-solving opportunity into an exercise in common denominators. I must figure out what more I can do to heighten my students' sense of adventure in mathematics. I want to increase my students' belief in their own mathematical power. I want them to search for mathematical connections and look for opportunities to apply new techniques in new situations. I don't want them to continue perceiving my problems as exercises to be quickly completed and checked off.

Suggested Reading

Steffe, L. P. 1990. "Adaptive Mathematics Teaching." In *Teaching and Learning Mathematics in the 1990s*, edited by T. J. Cooney and C. R. Hirsch, 41–51. Reston, VA: The National Council of Teachers of Mathematics.

The Ratio of Girls to Boys

We often hold discussions in my seventh-grade class, and sometimes I find myself totally unprepared for the questions my students ask. It's not that I feel I should be the one with the answers, but I do want to guide the discussion productively.

In a recent lesson introducing ratio concepts, I had written the fraction $\frac{1}{2}$ on the board and reminded my students that it meant "1 divided by 2," and that it also meant "1 out of 2."

"It is a division problem and also a ratio because it shows a comparison of 2 numbers—1 and 2," I explained. "Let's compare the number of boys and girls in our class." The class determined that there were 17 girls and 15 boys present.

"What is the ratio of girls to boys?"

Several students called out, "Seventeen to 15." I wrote the fraction $\frac{17}{15}$ on the board.

Carmen blurted out, "That can't be right. You said a fraction means the top divided by the bottom. That'll be more than 1 whole class."

Laura interjected, "And you said you could say 'out of'—like 17 out of 15. That doesn't sound right—17 girls out of 15 boys."

I realized that I wasn't very clear myself about how fractions and ratios were related or what part context plays in describing ratios. These were good questions and I wasn't sure how to handle them.

Suggested Reading

Cramer, K., and T. Post. 1993. "Making Connections: A Case for Proportionality." *Arithmetic Teacher* 40(6): 342–346.

Appendix

Advisory Board Members
Mathematics Case Methods Project

Phil Daro, Executive Director, California Mathematics Project, University of California Office of the President; Director for Assessment Development, New Standards Project, University of California Office of the President.

Lise Dworkin, Director, San Francisco Mathematics Collaborative.

Donna Goldenstein, Elementary Teacher, Hayward Unified School District.

Babette Jackson, Principal, Hayward Unified School District.

Carol Langbort, Chair, Department of Elementary Education, San Francisco State University.

Maisha Moses, Site Developer, The Algebra Project.

Judy Mumme, Director, Math Renaissance.

Sharon Ross, Professor, Department of Mathematics, California State University, Chico.

Jay Rowley, Principal, San Ramon Valley Unified School District.

Lee Shulman, Charles E. Ducommun Professor of Education, Stanford University.

Judy Shulman, Director, Institute for Case Development, Far West Laboratory.

Hardy Turrentine, Intermediate Teacher, Hayward Unified School District.

References

Allinger, G. D., and J. N. Payne. 1986. "Estimation and Mental Arithmetic with Percent." In *Estimation and Mental Computation*, edited by H. L. Schoen and M. J. Zweng, 141–155. Reston, VA: The National Council of Teachers of Mathematics.

Azzolino, A. 1990. "Writing as a Tool for Teaching Mathematics: The Silent Revolution." In *Teaching and Learning Mathematics in the 1990s*, edited by T. J. Cooney and C. R. Hirsch, 92–100. Reston, VA: The National Council of Teachers of Mathematics.

Ball, D. L. 1991. "'What's All This Talk About Discourse?': Implementing the Professional Standards for Teaching Mathematics." *Arithmetic Teacher* 39(8): 14–48.

Baroody, A. J. 1989. "Manipulatives Don't Come with Guarantees." *Arithmetic Teacher* 37(2): 4–5.

Behr, M. J., T. R. Post, and I. Wachsmuth. 1986. "Estimation and Children's Concept of Rational Number Size." In *Estimation and Mental Computation*, edited by H. L. Schoen and M. J. Zweng, 103–111. Reston, VA: The National Council of Teachers of Mathematics.

Beyer, B. 1983. "Common Sense About Teaching Skills." *Educational Leadership* 41(3): 44–49.

Borasi, R. 1990. "The Invisible Hand Operating in Mathematics Instruction: Students' Conceptions and Expectations." In *Teaching and Learning Mathematics in the 1990s*, edited by T. J. Cooney and C. R. Hirsch, 174–182. Reston, VA: The National Council of Teachers of Mathematics.

Carter, H. L. 1986. "Linking Estimation to Psychological Variables in the Early Years." In *Estimation and Mental Computation*, edited by H. L. Schoen and M. J. Zweng, 74–81. Reston, VA: The National Council of Teachers of Mathematics.

Clarke, D. J., D. M. Clarke, and C. J. Lovitt. 1990. "Changes in Mathematics Teaching Call for Assessment Alternatives." In *Teaching and Learning Mathematics in the 1990s*, edited by T. J. Cooney and C. R. Hirsch, 118–129. Reston, VA: The National Council of Teachers of Mathematics.

Cramer, K., and T. Post. 1993. "Making Connections: A Case for Proportionality." *Arithmetic Teacher* 40(6): 342–346.

Cuevas, G. 1990. "Increasing the Achievement and Participation of Language Minority Students in Mathematics Education." In *Teaching and Learning Mathematics in the 1990s*, edited by T. J. Cooney and C. R. Hirsch, 159–165. Reston, VA: The National Council of Teachers of Mathematics.

Curcio, F. R. 1990. "Mathematics as Communication: Using a Language-Experience Approach in the Elementary Grades." In *Teaching and Learning Mathematics in the 1990s,* edited by T. J. Cooney and C. R. Hirsch, 69–75. Reston, VA: The National Council of Teachers of Mathematics.

Damarin, S. K. 1990. "Teaching Mathematics: A Feminist Perspective." In *Teaching and Learning Mathematics in the 1990s,* edited by T. J. Cooney and C. R. Hirsch, 144–151. Reston, VA: The National Council of Teachers of Mathematics.

Donovan, B. F. 1990. "Cultural Power and the Defining of School Mathematics: A Case Study." In *Teaching and Learning Mathematics in the 1990s,* edited by T. J. Cooney and C. R. Hirsch, 166–173. Reston, VA: The National Council of Teachers of Mathematics.

Driscoll, M. and B. Lord. 1990. "Professionals in a Changing Profession." In *Teaching and Learning Mathematics in the 1990s,* edited by T. J. Cooney and C. R. Hirsch, 237–245. Reston, VA: The National Council of Teachers of Mathematics.

Hiebert, J. 1984. "Children's Mathematical Learning: The Struggle to Link Form and Understanding." *The Elementary School Journal* 84(5): 497–513.

Hiebert, J. 1990. "The Role of Routine Procedures in the Development of Mathematical Competence." In *Teaching and Learning Mathematics in the 1990s,* edited by T. J. Cooney and C. R. Hirsch, 31–40. Reston, VA: The National Council of Teachers of Mathematics.

Hiebert, J. 1992. "Mathematical, Cognitive, and Instructional Analyses of Decimal Fractions." In *Analysis of Arithmetic for Mathematics Teaching,* edited by G. Leinhardt, R. Putnam, and R. A. Hattrup, 283–322. Hillsdale, NJ: Lawrence Erlbaum Associates.

Holmes, E. E. 1990. "Motivation: An Essential Component of Mathematics Instruction." In *Teaching and Learning Mathematics in the 1990s,* edited by T. J. Cooney and C. R. Hirsch, 101–107. Reston, VA: The National Council of Teachers of Mathematics.

Janvier, C. 1990. "Contextualization and Mathematics for All." In *Teaching and Learning Mathematics in the 1990s,* edited by T. J. Cooney and C. R. Hirsch, 183–193. Reston, VA: The National Council of Teachers of Mathematics.

Kamii, C. 1990. "Constructivism and Beginning Arithmetic, K–12." In *Teaching and Learning Mathematics in the 1990s,* edited by T. J. Cooney and C. R. Hirsch, 22–30. Reston, VA: The National Council of Teachers of Mathematics.

Long, M. J., and M. Ben-Hur. 1991. "Informing Learning Through the Clinical Interview." *Arithmetic Teacher* 38(6): 44–46.

Miller, L. D. 1993. "Making the Connection with Language." *Arithmetic Teacher* 40(6): 311–316.

National Council of Teachers of Mathematics. 1989. *Curriculum and Evaluation Standards for School Mathematics.* Reston, VA: The National Council of Teachers of Mathematics.

National Council of Teachers of Mathematics. 1991. *Professional Standards for Teaching Mathematics.* Reston, VA: The National Council of Teachers of Mathematics.

Passmore, J. 1967. "On Teaching to Be Critical." In *The Concept of Education,* edited by R. S. Peters. London: Routledge & Kegan Paul.

Rowan, T. E., and N. D. Cetorelli. 1990. "An Eclectic Model for Teaching Elementary School Mathematics." In *Teaching and Learning Mathematics in the 1990s,* edited by T. J. Cooney and C. R. Hirsch, 62–68. Reston, VA: The National Council of Teachers of Mathematics.

Schielack, J. F. 1991. "Reaching Young Pupils with Technology." *Arithmetic Teacher* 38(6): 51–55.

Secada, W. G. 1990. "The Challenges of a Changing World for Mathematics Education." In *Teaching and Learning Mathematics in the 1990s,* edited by T. J. Cooney and C. R. Hirsch, 135–143. Reston, VA: The National Council of Teachers of Mathematics.

Steen, L. A. 1990. "Mathematics for All Americans." In *Teaching and Learning Mathematics in the 1990s,* edited by T. J. Cooney and C. R. Hirsch, 130–134. Reston, VA: The National Council of Teachers of Mathematics.

Steffe, L. P. 1990. "Adaptive Mathematics Teaching." In *Teaching and Learning Mathematics in the 1990s,* edited by T. J. Cooney and C. R. Hirsch, 41–51. Reston, VA: The National Council of Teachers of Mathematics.

Stigler, J. W. 1988. "Research into Practice: The Use of Verbal Explanation in Japanese and American Classrooms." *Arithmetic Teacher* 36(2): 27–29.

Stigler, J. W. and H. W. Stevenson. 1991. "How Asian Teachers Polish Each Lesson to Perfection." *American Educator* 15(1): 12–47.

Sullivan, P., and D. Clarke. 1991. "Catering to All Abilities Through 'Good' Questions." *Arithmetic Teacher* 39(2): 14–18.

Webb, N., and D. Briars. 1990. "Assessment in Mathematics Classrooms, K–8." In *Teaching and Learning Mathematics in the 1990s,* edited by T. J. Cooney and C. R. Hirsch, 108–117. Reston, VA: The National Council of Teachers of Mathematics.

Wilde, S. 1991. "Learning to Write About Mathematics." *Arithmetic Teacher* 38(6): 38–43.

Witherspoon, M. 1993. "Fractions: In Search of Meaning." *Arithmetic Teacher* 40(8): 482–485.

Woodcock, G. E. 1986. "Estimating Fractions: A Picture is Worth a Thousand Words." In *Estimation and Mental Computation,* edited by H. L. Schoen and M. J. Zweng, 112–115. Reston, VA: The National Council of Teachers of Mathematics.

Yackel, E., P. Cobb, T. Wood, G. Wheatley, and G. Merkel. 1990. "The Importance of Social Interaction in Children's Construction of Mathematical Knowledge." In *Teaching and Learning Mathematics in the 1990s,* edited by T. J. Cooney and C. R. Hirsch, 12–21. Reston, VA: The National Council of Teachers of Mathematics.

For additional information about facilitator preparation and case-writing semi-nars, or to be placed on a mailing list for future publications of casebooks, contact:

Carne Barnett
Mathematics Case Methods Project
Far West Laboratory
730 Harrison Street
San Francisco, CA 94107-1242
Fax: 415-565-3012